THE NEW MAN

The New Man

THOMAS MERTON

BURNS & OATES
A Continuum imprint
LONDON • NEW YORK

Burns & Oates
A Continuum imprint

The Tower Building   15 East 26th Street
11 York Road   New York 10010
London SE1 7NX
www.continuumbooks.com

First published in Great Britain in 1962

This edition published in 1976
Reprinted 1985, 1991, 1996, 2003

Copyright © 1961 by the
Abbey of Our Lady of Gethsemani

ISBN 0 8601 2344 8

Printed and bound in Great Britain by
Biddles Ltd, *www.biddles.co.uk*

CONTENTS

PART I

THE WAR WITHIN US

* I *

LIFE and death are at war within us. As soon as we are
born, we begin at the same time to live and die.

Even though we may not be even slightly aware of it, this
battle of life and death goes on in us inexorably and without
mercy. If by chance we become fully conscious of it, not
only in our flesh and in our emotions but above all in our
spirit, we find ourselves involved in a terrible wrestling, an
agonia not of questions and answers, but of being and
nothingness, spirit and void. In this most terrible of all wars,
fought on the brink of infinite despair, we come gradually
to realize that life is more than the reward for him who
correctly guesses a secret and spiritual "answer" to which he
smilingly remains committed. This is more than a matter of
"finding peace of mind," or "settling religious problems."

Indeed, for the man who enters into the black depths of
the *agonia*, religious problems become an unthinkable
luxury. He has no time for such indulgences. He is fighting
for his life. His being itself is a foundering ship, ready with
each breath to plunge into nothingness and yet inexplicably
remaining afloat on the void. Questions that have answers
seem, at such a time, to be a cruel mockery of the helpless
mind. Existence itself becomes an absurd question, like a
Zen *koan*: and to find an answer to such a question is to be
irrevocably lost. An absurd question can have only an absurd
answer.

Religions do not, in fact, simply supply answers to
questions. Or at least they do not confine themselves to
this until they become degenerate. Salvation is more than

I

the answer to a question. To emerge alive from a disaster is not just the answer to the question, "Shall I escape?"

Everything hangs on the final issue, in the battle of life and death. Nothing is assured beforehand. Nothing is definitely certain. The issue is left to our own choice. But that is what constitutes the dark terror of the *agonia*: we cannot be sure of our own choice. Are we strong enough to continue choosing life when to live means to go on and on with this absurd battle of entity and nonentity in our own inmost self?

The roots of life remain immortal and invulnerable in us if we will continue to keep morally alive by hope. Yet hope in its full supernatural dimension is beyond our pwer. And when we try to keep ourselves in hope by sheer violent persistence in willing to live, we end if not in despair in what is worse—delusion. (For in reality such delusion is a despair that refuses to take cognizance of itself. It is the merciful form which cowards give to their despair.)

Hope then is a gift. Like life, it is a gift from God, total, unexpected, incomprehensible, undeserved. It springs out of nothingness, completely free. But to meet it, we have to descend into nothingness. And there we meet hope most perfectly, when we are stripped of our own confidence, our own strength, when we almost no longer exist. "A hope that is seen," says St. Paul, "is no hope." No hope. Therefore despair. To *see* your hope is to abandon hope.

The Christian hope that is "not seen" is a communion in the agony of Christ. It is the identification of our own *agonia* with the *agonia* of the God Who has emptied Himself and become obedient unto death. It is the acceptance of life in the midst of death, not because we have courage, or light, or wisdom to accept, but because by some miracle the

God of Life Himself accepts to live, in us, at the very moment when we descend into death.

All truly religious thought claims to arm man for his struggle with death with weapons that will ensure the victory of life over death.

* 2 *

THE most paradoxical and at the same time the most unique and characteristic claim made by Christianity is that in the Resurrection of Christ the Lord from the dead, man has completely conquered death, and that "in Christ" the dead will rise again to enjoy eternal life, in spiritualized and transfigured bodies and in a totally new creation. This new life in the Kingdom of God is to be not merely a passively received inheritance but in some sense the fruit of our agony and labour, love and prayers in union with the Holy Spirit. Such a fantastic and humanly impossible belief has generally been left in the background by the liberal Christianity of the 19th and early 20th centuries, but anyone who reads the New Testament objectively must admit that this is the doctrine of the first Christians. Indeed, Christianity without this fabulous eschatological claim is only a moral system without too much spiritual consistency. Unless all Christianity is centred in the victorious, living, and ever present reality of Jesus Christ, the Man-God and conqueror of death, it loses its distinctive character and there is no longer any justification for a Christian missionary apostolate. In point of fact, such an apostolate, without the resurrection of the dead, has tended to be purely and simply an apostolate for western cultural and economic "progress," and not a true preaching of the Gospel.

The fullness of human life cannot be measured by anything that happens only to the body. Life is not merely a matter of physical vigour, or of health, or of the capacity to enjoy oneself. What is life? It is something far more than the breath in our nostrils, the blood beating in our wrists, the response to physical stimulation. True, all these things are essential for a fully human life, but they do not themselves constitute that life in all its fullness. A man can have all this and still be an idiot. And one who merely breathes, eats, sleeps and works, without awareness, without purpose and without ideas of his own is not really a man. Life, in this purely physical sense, is merely the absence of death. Such people do not live, they vegetate.

For a man to be alive, he must exercise not only the acts that belong to vegetative and animal life, he must not only subsist, grow, be sentient, not only move himself around, feed himself, and the rest. He must carry on the activities proper to his own specifically human kind of life. He must, that is to say, think intelligently. And above all he must direct his actions by free decisions, made in the light of his own thinking. They must tend to make him more aware of his capacities for knowledge and for free action. They must expand and extend his power to love others, and to dedicate himself to their good: for it is in this that he finds his own fulfilment.

In a word, for man to live, he has to become wholly and entirely alive. He has to be all life, in his body, his senses, his mind and his will.

But this life must also have a certain special order and coherence. We often see people who are said to be "bursting with life" and who, in fact, are simply wrestling with their own incoherence.

Life, indeed, is meant to superabound but not to explode.

4

Those who are bursting with life are often merely plunging into death with an enormous splash. They do not transcend death, they surrender to it with so much animal vitality that they are able to drag many others with them into the abyss.

* 3 *

IN those who are most alive and therefore most themselves, the life of the body is subordinated to a higher life that is within them. It quietly surrenders to the far more abundant vitality of a spirit living on levels that defy measurement and observation. The mark of true life in man is therefore not turbulence but control, not effervescence but lucidity and direction, not passion but the sobriety that sublimates all passion and elevates it to the clear inebriation of mysticism. The control we mean here is not arbitrary and tyrannical control by an interior principle which can be called, variously, a "super-ego" or a pharisaical conscience: it is the harmonious coordination of man's powers in striving for the realization of his deepest spiritual potentialities. It is not so much a control of one part of man by another, but the peaceful integration of all man's powers into one perfect actuality which is his true self, that is to say his spiritual self.

Man, then, can only fully be said to be alive when he becomes plainly conscious of the real meaning of his own existence, that is to say when he *experiences* something of the fullness of intelligence, freedom and spirituality that are actualized within himself.

But can we really expect a man to attain to this kind of consciousness? Is it not utterly cruel to hold before his eyes the delusive hope of this "fullness" of life and of "realization"? Of course, if the nature of the hope is not understood, it is the cruellest and most mocking of delusions. It may be the worst of all spiritual mirages that torments him in his desert pilgrimage. How can a man, plunged in the *agonia*, the wrestling of life and death in their most elemental spiritual forms, be beguiled by the promise of self-realization? His very self, his very reality, is all contradiction: a contradiction mercifully obscured by confusion. If the confusion is cleared away, and he fully "realizes" this tormented self, what will he see if not the final absurdity of the contradiction? The "real meaning of his existence" would then be precisely that it has no meaning.

In a certain sense, that is true. To find life we must die to life as we know it. To find meaning we must die to meaning as we know it. The sun rises every morning and we are used to it, and because we know the sun will rise we have finally come to act as if it rose because we wanted it to. Suppose the sun should choose not to rise? Some of our mornings would then be "absurd"—or, to put it mildly, they would not meet our expectations.

To find the full meaning of our existence we must find not the meaning that we expect but the meaning that is revealed to us by God. The meaning that comes to us out of the transcendent darkness of His mystery and our own. We do not know God and we do not know ourselves. How then can we imagine that it is possible for us to chart our own course toward the discovery of the meaning of our life? This meaning is not a sun that rises every morning, though we have come to think that it does, and on mornings when it does not rise we substitute some artificial light of our own so as not to admit that this morning was absurd.

Meaning is then not something we discover in ourselves, or in our lives. The meanings we are capable of discovering are never sufficient. The true meaning has to be revealed. It has to be "given." And the fact that it is given is, indeed, the greater part of its significance: for life itself is, in the end, only significant in so far as it is given.

As long as we experience life and existence as suns that have to rise every morning, we are in agony. We must learn that life is a light that rises when God summons it out of darkness. For this there are no fixed times.

* 4 *

MAN is fully alive only when he experiences, at least to some extent, that he is really spontaneously dedicating himself, in all truth, to the real purpose of his own personal existence. In other words, man is alive not only when he exists and acts as man (that is to say freely), but above all when he is conscious of the reality and inviolability of his own freedom, and aware at the same time of his capacity to consecrate that freedom entirely to the purpose for which it was given him.

And this realization does not come into being until his freedom is actually devoted to its right purpose. Man "finds himself" and is happy, when he is able to be aware that his freedom is spontaneously and vigorously functioning to orientate his whole being toward the purpose which it craves, in its deepest spiritual centre, to achieve. This purpose is *life* in the fullest sense of the word—not mere individual, self-centred, egotistical life which is doomed to end in death, but a life that transcends individual limitations and needs, and subsists outside the individual self in the Absolute—in Christ, in God.

Man is truly alive when he is aware of himself as the master of his own destiny to life or to death, aware of the fact that his ultimate fulfilment or destruction depends on his own free choice and aware of his ability to decide for himself. This is the beginning of true life.

Yet, once again, this is theory and ideal. What is the reality? Fallen man in whom life and death are fighting for mastery is no longer fully master of himself: he has no power left except to cry out for help in the void. Help, it is true, comes as an unaccountable answer to his cry, though never in the form that he expects. Can this be called "mastery"? Paradoxically, it is here and here alone that man has mastery over his spiritual destiny. It is here that he chooses. It is here that his freedom, in its despairing struggle for survival, is "spontaneously and vigorously functioning to orient his whole being to the purpose which it craves." How careful we must be with these sanguine metaphors of power and self-realization. Man's real power lies hidden in the agony which makes him cry out to God: and there he is at the same time helpless and omnipotent. He is utterly helpless in himself, and yet he can "do all things in the Invisible who strengthens him."

> *Circumdederunt me!* . . .
> The sorrows of hell came up all around me
> death bundled me up in a net
> in my bitter struggle I cried out to the Lord
> and I called to my God
> and from His holy temple He heard my voice,
> my cry came up and He looked at it
> and it went in by His ears. . . .
> He bowed down the heavens and descended
> with darkness under His feet.
> He rode upon the cherubs and flew,
> flew on the flying wind,
> and made Himself a hiding place in darkness
> darkness all around Him like a tent! . . .

He reached down from the far heights and took me,
and pulled me out of the waterfloods.
[Psalm 17, from the Vulgate].

True life, in other words, is not vegetative subsistence in
one's own self, nor animal self-assertion and self-gratifica-
tion. It is freedom transcending the self and subsisting in
"the other" by love. It is entirely received from God. It is a
freedom which "loses its life in order to find it," instead of
saving its own life and thereby losing it. The perfection of
life is spiritual love. And Christianity believes so firmly
in the power of love, in the Holy Spirit, that it asserts divine
love can even overcome death. And it risks death in order to
experience the fullness of life.

But the summit of life, in man, is also contemplation.
Contemplation is the perfection of love and of knowledge.
Man's life grows and is made perfect by those acts in which
his enlightened intelligence takes hold of truth, and by those
even more important acts in which his inviolable freedom
as it were absorbs and assimilates the truth by love, and
makes his own soul true by "doing the truth in charity."
Contemplation is the coalescence of life, knowledge,
freedom, and love in a supremely simple intuition of the
unity of all love, freedom, truth and life in their source,
which is God.

* 5 *

Contemplation is at once the existential appreciation of
our own "nothingness" and of the divine reality, perceived
by ineffable spiritual contact within the depths of our own
being. Contemplation is the sudden intuitive penetration of
what really IS. It is the unexpected leap of the spirit of man
into the existential luminosity of Reality Itself, not merely

9

by the metaphysical intuition of being, but by the transcendent fulfilment of an existential communion with Him Who IS.

This is what makes the mystic far more existential than the philosopher. For where the true metaphysician turns aside from the pure objective concept of being as such in order to grasp being subjectively by experience and intuition, the mystic goes further still and plunges into the dynamic infinity of a Reality which not only IS, but which pours forth from its own inexhaustible depths the reality of everything else that is real. The mystic, that is to say the contemplative, not only sees and touches what is real, but beyond the surface of all that is actual, he attains to communion with the Freedom Who is the source of all actuality. This Reality, this Freedom, is not concept, not a thing, not an object, not even an object of knowledge: it is the Living God, the Holy One, the One to Whom we dare to utter a Name only because He has revealed a Name to us, but Who is behind all names as He is beyond all being, beyond all knowing, beyond all loving. He is the infinitely Other, the Transcendent, of Whom we have and can have no univocal idea. He is so far above being that it is in some sense truer to say of Him that He "is not" than that He is. Yet at the same time we best name Him Who is the fullness of life by saying that He IS. And He Who IS (or "is not," depending whether you look at it apophatically or cataphatically) dwells at the very heart of our own being. The pure summit of our own actuality is the threshold of His Sanctuary, and He is nearer to us than we are to ourselves.

* 6 *

IT is in this perfect self-realization by contact of our own anguished freedom with the life-giving Freedom of Him Who is Holy and Unknown that man begins the conquest of death in his own soul. This finding of our true self, this awakening, this coming to life in the luminous darkness of the infinite God, can never be anything but a communion with God by the grace of Jesus Christ. Our victory over death is not our own work, but His. The triumph of our own freedom, which must truly be *our* triumph if it is to save us from death, is nevertheless also and primarily His. And consequently, in all these meditations we will be talking of contemplation as a sharing in the death and Resurrection of Christ. The Church sings, in the Easter Sequence, how "life and death met in an amazing battle," and how "the Prince of Life, Who died, lives and reigns."

> Mors et vita duello
> Conflixere mirando:
> Dux vitae mortuus
> Regnat vivus.

This victory of life over death which was won by the Author of Life is the very soul of the ancient and traditional existentialism of the Church—an existentialism so calmly and obviously existential that it never needed to be called by such a name.

Christian contemplation is existential not only in the sense that it experiences our own reality immersed in the reality of Him Who IS, but also in the sense that it is the participation in a concrete action of God in time, the climax of the divine irruption into human history which, because it was an act of God as well as of Man, is capable of communicating itself spiritually and repeating itself over and over again in the lives of individual men.

* 7 *

CONTEMPLATION is a mark of a fully mature Christian life. It makes the believer no longer a slave or a servant of a Divine Master, no longer the fearful keeper of a difficult law, no longer even an obedient and submissive son who is still too young to participate in his Father's counsels. Contemplation is that wisdom which makes man the friend of God, a thing which Aristotle thought to be impossible. For how, he said, can a man be God's friend? Friendship implies equality. That is precisely the message of the Gospel:

No longer do I call you servants, because the servant does not know what his master does. But I have called you friends, because all things that I have heard from my Father I have made known to you. You have not chosen me, but I have chosen you, and have appointed you that you should go and bear fruit, and that your fruit should remain; that whatever you ask the Father in my name he may give you. . . . I am the vine, you are the branches. He who abides in me, and I in him, he bears much fruit; for without me you can do nothing. . . . If you abide in me, and if my words abide in you, ask whatever you will, and it shall be done to you. [John 15: 15-16, 5, 7.]

If we are the sons of God, then we are "heirs also," co-heirs with Christ our brother. The heir is one who has a right to his Father's possessions. Whoever has the fullness of Christian life is no longer a dog eating the crumbs under the Father's table, but a son who sits and banquets with the Father. This is precisely the lot of the mature Christian, for by the Ascension of Christ, as St. Paul says, "God has made us sit together with Him in the heavenly places." [Ephesians 2: 6.]

* 8 *

CONTEMPLATION is a foretaste of the definitive victory of life over death in our souls. Without contemplation we indeed *believe* in the possibility of this victory, and we *hope* for it. But when our love for God bursts out into the dark yet luminous flame of interior vision, we are enabled, at least for an instant, to experience something of the victory. For at such moments "life" and "reality" and "God" cease to be concepts which we think about and become realities in which we consciously participate.

The reality of God is known to us in contemplation in an entirely new way. When we apprehend God through the medium of concepts, we see Him as an object separate from ourselves, as a being from whom we are alienated, even though we believe that He loves us and that we love Him. In contemplation this division disappears, for contemplation goes beyond concepts and apprehends God not as a separate object but as the Reality within our own reality, the Being within our being, the life of our life. In order to express this reality we have to use symbolic language, and in respecting the metaphysical distinction between the Creator and creature we have to emphasize the I-Thou relationship between the soul and God. Nevertheless, the experience of contemplation is the experience of God's life and presence within ourselves not as object but as the transcendent source of our own subjectivity. Contemplation is a mystery in which God reveals Himself to us as the very centre of our own most intimate self—*intimior intimo meo* as St. Augustine said. When the realization of His presence bursts upon us, our own self disappears in Him and we pass mystically through the Red Sea of separation to lose ourselves (and thus find our true selves) in Him.

Contemplation is the highest and most paradoxical form of self-realization, attained by apparent self-annihilation.

Life, then, is not only known, but *lived*. It is lived and

experienced in its completeness, that is to say in all the ramifications of its spiritual activity. All the powers of the soul reach out in freedom and knowledge and love, and all converge again, and all are gathered together in one supreme act which is radiant with peace. The concreteness of this experience of reality is in the highest sense existential. And furthermore it is a communion—a perception of our own reality immersed in and in some sense coalescent with the supreme Reality, the Infinite Act of Existing we call God. Finally, it is a communion with Christ, the incarnate Word. Not only a personal union of souls with Him, but a communion in the one great act by which He conquered death once and for all in His death and Resurrection.

* 9 *

THERE is a Promethean mysticism which is a struggle with the gods, and because it is a struggle with the gods it seems great to those who do not know the Living God. What did Prometheus do? He stole fire from the gods, and they punished him for it. Hesiod's version of the myth of Prometheus is the image of man's psychological situation: guilty, rebellious, frustrated, unsure of himself, of his gifts and of his own strength, alienated, yet seeking to assert himself. He sees the battle between life and death in a wrong perspective. His vision is a vision of defeat and despair. Life cannot win against death, for the gods have all the power in their hands and they must live on while we die. For us, then, there is only one issue from the struggle—a glorious defiance in the assertion of our despair. Prometheus is not the symbol of victory but of defeat. Promethean mysticism has precisely this negative quality about it: since it cannot conceive of a true victory, it makes a victory out of defeat and glories in its own despair. But this is only because Prometheus believes in death rather than life. He is convinced, in advance, that he must die.

* 10 *

THE Promethean instinct is as deep as man's weakness. That is to say it is almost infinite. It has its roots in the bottomless abyss of man's own nothingness. It is the despairing cry that rises out of the darkness of man's metaphysical solitude—the inarticulate expression of a terror man will not admit to himself: his terror at having to be himself, at having to be a person. For the fire Prometheus steals from the gods is his own incommunicable reality, his own spirit. It is the affirmation and vindication of his own being. Yet this being is a gift of God, and it does not have to be stolen. It can only be had by a free gift—the very hope of gaining it by theft is pure illusion.

* II *

NOT knowing that the fire was his for the asking, not knowing that fire was something that God did not need, something that God had created expressly for man, Prometheus felt he had to steal it. But why? Because he knew no god that would be willing to give it to him for nothing. He knew no god that was not an enemy, because the only gods he knew were only a little stronger than himself. He had to steal the fire from gods that were weak. If he had known the strong God, everything would have been quite different.

* 12 *

IF we look closely at this theft of fire, we see that it was in the end not so much a gesture of defiance as an act of adoration. It was almost as if Prometheus had stolen the fire in order to give it back to his gods; as if he were coming to them with the flames in his hands like vivid and sentient flowers, instead of flying from them with his life flickering between his fingers.

How sad is the figure of Prometheus and how sad are his gods: for they had to fear him in order to exist and he had to hate them in order to live. Who cannot see that Prometheus and his guilt and his gods are simply the composite picture of man's own schizophrenia? Why must we live in the shadow-kingdom of beings who can never quite believe that they themselves exist? Without the living God (without a centre) men become little helpless gods, imprisoned within the four walls of their own weakness and fear. They are so conscious of their weakness that they think they have nothing to give to another, and that they can only subsist by snatching from others the little they have, a little love, a little knowledge, a little power. So from the very beginning their lives are a constant apology: "I am sorry, father, mother, but in growing up I must steal your fire. You are weak gods, and I love you, but you are right to fear me as I know you do. For you decrease and I must increase, and I must grow and live on your decline. I wish it were otherwise. But since things are as they are, you must inevitably fear me under the cloak of love and I must love you as the result of fear, for we are guilty before one another, and none of us has any right to exist at all. . . ."

The father fights his son in order that the son may not grow up and condemn the father. The mother shall be jealous of the daughter and shall spite her, for fear of being, in her own turn, rejected. (Or else, if they are all conscientious, they hide their secret fear under attachments to one another that are more unbreakable than despair itself —as if the child, to prove over and over again his submission to his mother, were resolutely to refuse to issue from her womb.)

Such are the deep roots of the Promethean instinct which passes for heroism among men.

* 13 *

PROMETHEUS is the mystic without faith, who believes neither in himself nor in God. And when I call him a mystic, I use the term in a facetious sense:—the man who needs

17

fire from outside himself is in a certain sense condemned to live out his life in the hope of some impossible ecstasy. For Prometheus, this ecstasy is an apparent success, for he steals fire and he achieves that ecstasy of punishment by which the theft is justified and explained.

If a Prometheus happens to appear, here and there, among the men of our time, he looms over them like a giant among pygmies. They envy his magnificent and public chastisement. They think he is the person they do not dare to be. He has defied heaven, and his punishment remains as an eternal reproach to the gods. He has had the last word!

＊ 14 ＊

PROMETHEUS transcends ordinary men by the intensity and power of his egoism, by the glamour of his adventure and by the violence of his self-hate. He has dared to reach down into the depths of his own spirit and find the forbidden, existential fire. They, in their turn, do not dare to seek or to find it because they are incapable of so great an illusion of guilt. He will find it for them and he, at the same time, will endure the envied punishment. They will stand by in sorrow, and admire.

＊ 15 ＊

PROMETHEUS is the prophet and contemplative that is required by the atomic age. He is the symbol and scapegoat who justifies our momentous discoveries by his death-mysticism. As long as we do not have the courage to use well what we have discovered, as long as we feel compelled to use everything badly and turn all our power to our own destruction, Prometheus has to be nailed to the cliff in front of us to explain why. We have to be destroyed because we are nothing, because we never existed anyway, because we have no right to be persons, because the affronted gods are jealous of us.

Let us not be too quick to say that the greatness of Prometheus is altogether an illusion. In relation to the rest of men, he is indeed a giant. For he who has the courage to scale a mountain, even though the scaling be utterly useless, has at least a certain advantage over those who remain in the plain. He has the courage to admit that he is afraid, and he has the courage to do the thing they are all afraid of.

* 16 *

If Prometheus seems greater than the "right thinking" herd at the bottom of the mountain, it is because he is to some extent more honest than they in his illusions. They claim to love the gods and to respect them. He admits he is afraid of them. They claim they can do without fire—that is to say, they are content not to exist, or to exist in a numbness without pain. He, on the contrary, determines to attack the problem of his own existence head-on, and demand that the gods tell him why he is not a person. And he has a certain right to be jealous of an answer which he thinks he has stolen from the summit of an Olympus which he found, to his surprise, to be without the gods he feared to find there. And so, finally, he marches off to Caucasus of his own accord, and chains himself to the rock, and calls for his pain and his vulture. Nor is it the vulture that is inexorable, but Prometheus, who insists that the bird be there. And so he stands and suffers, with a sorrow that is at once monumental and absurd, punishing and pitying himself because there are no gods and because he, who wants to be his own god, realizes that he can only be so by being punished.

19

Lᴇᴛ all right thinking people avoid the smoking mountain
of this new Moses, and fear to accept his law which is a
non-law, his freedom to be more enslaved by guilt than
would ever have been possible if the law had not been
abolished. Let them prefer to pretend that there is fire to be
stolen, that there are powers who will resent and punish
the stealing of the fire. Let them claim that the world has a
definite meaning: but that they do not want to know what
the meaning is. Let them claim that life has its obligations:
but that they do not want to find out what these may be.
They assert that the gods are all quite real, but they do not
want to have anything to do, one way or the other, with
divinity. Rightness, piety, justice, religion, consist, for
them, in the definition of various essences. Not only that,
but justice demands, in their eyes, that essence should not be
tainted with existence.

If only these right thinking men could taste something of
Prometheus's real despair, we would imagine them for a
moment worthy of honour. But they are worthy of no
honour at all, only of disdain. For where the rightness of
Prometheus consists in wanting to be wrong, as if being
wrong were the only way of vindicating what is right; the
rightness of the "right thinking" man is, on the other hand,
an essence which does not have to exist. Therefore the right
thinking really need have no concern with actual right or
wrong. In this they resemble Prometheus, but they do not
bother to make it a matter for suffering, or for defiance, or
even for comment. The piety of Prometheus consists in a
despairing rebellion against his gods, a rebellion which is
born of love for them. The piety of the "right thinking"
man is a secret determination to ignore the gods altogether,

or to recognize them only with outward formalities which are understood in advance to mean nothing at all. The religion of the right thinking man is satisfied with the *notion* of gods. (It is sufficient to pay homage to the notion, just in case the gods might turn out to have an existence after all.)

* 18 *

PROMETHEUS has at least this much justice: he insists on being punished. But the justice of these others consists in the subversion of all the most fundamental rights of man by a sentimentality (or a cynicism) which gives you a penny with one hand and, with the other, robs you of your immortal soul.

The right thinking man is like the poor: we have him always with us. He is the unbelieving believer: that is to say the religious man who lives, in practice, without a god. He is the one who pretends to believe, who acts as if he believes, who seems to be moral because he has a set of rigid principles. He clings to a certain number of fixed moral essences but at the same time he takes very good care never to ask himself whether or not they may be real. He will rob you and enslave you and murder you and give you a plausible reason for doing so. He always has a reason, even though his reasons may cancel one another out by a series of contradictions. That does not matter at all, since he does not need the truth, nor justice, nor mercy, least of all God: all he needs is "to be a right thinking man."

* 19 *

A KIND of schizophrenic self-alienation lies at the source of all the inadequate mysticisms of heroism and of guilt. The longing of the restless spirit of man, seeking to transcend itself by its own powers, is symbolized by the need to scale the impossible mountain and find there what is after all our own. When a man writes good poetry, it comes from within himself. But there have been poets who could only reach the sources within themselves when they thought they were defying the gods in order to drink from the hidden spring. And there are religious men who pray best when they imagine they are rejected by an angry and implacable God. Their prayer and their spirituality consist in the acceptance of apparent rejection. God Himself is less necessary to them than their sentiments of despair. He fits into their lives best when they are tortured by the revenging vulture. Underneath it all is the conviction that God cannot pardon them for wanting to live, for wanting to be perfect, and to be free. It is His grace, indeed, which fills them with the insatiable need for life. But their own strange natures only enable them to admit such a need when it is disguised, at the same time, as a need for punishment.

* 20 *

FROM the moment religious thought takes, as its starting point, the view that man has to achieve his salvation by stealing fire from heaven, it tends towards naturalism. Even the doctrinal systems which lean most heavily in favour of grace (like, for instance, Jansenism) are basically naturalistic because of their Promethean character.

Theology becomes Promethean whenever it assumes that man's supreme perfection is something God wants to prevent him from attaining. But this assumption is invariably accompanied by the secret conviction that this spiritual perfection is *of and for ourselves*. In other words, wherever we find a theology that is Promethean in character, that is to say that conceives salvation as a stealing of fire from heaven, we also find an implicit naturalism that sees our salvation and perfection in something other than God Himself.

For instance, it is very common to find, even under the formulas of impeccable orthodoxy, a raffishly Promethean spirituality which is avid not so much for God as for "spiritual perfection." The language of prayer in such cases may be the language of the most consummate humility. Grace becomes everything. Nature is worse than nothing: it is an abhorrent nothing. And yet such a spirituality may be completely self-centred. Its orientation can be *directly opposed* to the true orientation of Christianity. Instead of being the fulfilment of a Christian finding himself in God through the charity and selflessness of Jesus Christ, it becomes the rebellion of a Promethean soul who is trying to raid heaven and steal the divine fire for its own glorification. What Prometheus wants is not the glory of God but his own perfection. He has forgotten the terrible paradox that the only way we become perfect is by leaving ourselves, and, in a certain sense, forgetting our own perfection, to follow Christ.

* 21 *

THE great error of Promethean mysticism is that it takes no account of anyone but the self. For Prometheus, there is no "other." His spirit, his strivings, have no relation to any other person. Everything converges upon himself. But the secret of Christian mysticism is that it fulfils the self by selfless love for other persons.

After all, if our salvation consists in finding ourselves in God, it means finding ourselves to be as God is. But we only do this by being what God is and acting as He acts, which, of course, is impossible without His direct intervention. "You therefore are to be perfect, even as your heavenly Father is perfect. . . . Abide in me, and I in you. As the branch cannot bear fruit of itself unless it remain on the vine, so neither can you unless you abide in me." [Matt. 5: 48; John 15: 4.] And God, we read, is charity. Hence the folly of a mysticism which does not turn outward to the "other," but remains enclosed within itself. Such mysticism is simply an escape from reality: it barricades itself from the real and feeds upon itself.

One of the real reasons why Prometheus is condemned to be his own prisoner is because he is incapable of understanding the liberality of God. We have said before and we repeat it here again: the fire he thinks he has to steal is after all his own fire. God created this spiritual fire for His own sons—more than that, He gives them His own uncreated and sanctifying fire which is the Holy Spirit. But Prometheus, who does not understand liberality since he has none of it in himself, refuses the gift of God.

Here is the central reason for his inescapable feeling of guilt. He condemns himself to frustration. He cannot enjoy the gift of God unless he snatches it away when God is not looking. This is necessary, for Prometheus demands that the fire be his by right of conquest. Otherwise he will not believe it is really his own. And that is the paradox that St. Paul saw so clearly: salvation belongs to the order of love, of freedom and of giving. It is not ours if it is conquered, only if it is freely received, as it is freely given.

* 22 *

IN whatever forms it takes, Promethean spirituality is

24

obsessed with "mine" and "thine"—on the distinction between what is "mine" and what belongs to God. So it is the drive which urged the prodigal son to bring about a clear separation between the heritage that was "his" and the rest of his father's possessions. Now although it is quite true that among the gifts of nature and of grace with which we have been endowed, some can be said to belong more properly to us, others more exclusively to God, we must remember that the truth of Christian teaching culminates in the paradox that all that belongs to me is at the same time fully mine and fully God's.

The prodigal son takes his part of the inheritance, glad that it is *his*, and travels as far as he can from his father's house. Up to the point where the prodigal enters into himself and remembers where he came from, the story is that of Prometheus and the vulture. The prodigal has not stolen anything, but he thinks that to "find himself," he must segregate whatever can be classified as "his" and exploit it for his own self-affirmation. His selfishness and his withdrawal are like a theft of fire. His sojourn with the swine corresponds to the punishment of Prometheus devoured by the vulture. The prodigal's self-fulfilment, though not spectacular, is still Promethean.

* 23 *

THEOLOGICAL disputation about free will and grace, especially since the Reformation, has ended in many theologians unwittingly running off with the prodigal son. Once the question of grace and free will is reduced to a juridical matter, once witnesses line up with plaintiff or defendant and the jurors strive to determine who is entitled to what, we are inevitably tempted to act as if everything that was given to free will was taken from grace, and everything conceded to grace was withdrawn from our own liberty.

On both sides of the debate, whether one is arguing "for grace" or whether one is a defender of "nature," it seems that everyone is more or less obsessed with this great illusion of ownership and possession. *What is strictly mine?* How much can God demand of me—how much can I demand of Him? Even if I come up with the answer that nothing is strictly mine at all, I have still falsified the perspective by asking a foolish question in the first place. "How much is *mine?*" Should such a question ever be asked? Should such a division even be made at all? To ask such a question makes it almost impossible for me to grasp the paradox which is the only possible answer: That *everything is mine* precisely because *everything is His.* If it were not His, it could never be mine. If it could not be mine, He would not even want it for Himself. And all that is His, is His very self. All that He gives me becomes, in some way, my own self. What, then is mine? He is mine. And what is His? I am His. But when this becomes clear, there is no place left in the picture for anything resembling Prometheus.

Unless great care is taken, and unless the real theological issue is kept in sight, the argument, grace vs. free will, becomes a Promethean battle between man and God. It is true that the dramatic aspects of the struggle are left in the background, since the whole affair is treated less as a battle than as a lawsuit. But the fact remains that man begins to fix his attention on what God "*has to*" give him, and at the same time to measure up just how much he himself "has to" give to God in return.

In tallying up the account, how much is a free gift of God and how much is a payment due to us in strict justice? To what extent do we have to act like beggars? What do we have to pray for humbly, and when, if ever, can we throw our humility to the winds and make a categorical demand?

* 24 *

IN this atmosphere of theological litigation it comes to seem as if *God did not want us to be free*, as if freedom were something He envied and begrudged us; as if grace, while making us "safe," took all the sting out of this dangerous faculty of free will by robbing us of spontaneous initiative; in other words, it seems as if man saves himself and arrives at divine union by bartering his freedom for God's grace. The price of happiness is the renunciation of his natural autonomy, and the acceptance of a slave-status in the household of a God who is powerful enough to make slavery worth while. The extreme development of this view does not even leave man free to drive the necessary bargain. God simply makes an arbitrary decision to grant grace to this one and that one. The grace works infallibly. It takes away their free will and saves them in spite of themselves. They are bound hand and foot and thrown into the wedding banquet, no doubt to be fed through a tube.

* 25 *

AT the other extreme, with the Pelagians and their naturalistic successors, the process is more explicitly Promethean. God gives man the power of freedom and man, without any further help from God, except for the "good example" and the inspiration of Christ, works out his own salvation by heroic exploits without either fear or trembling. At first sight, this solution is the one which is most appealing to modern man. It makes him completely independent of God. He is responsible to no one but himself, and God becomes his debtor, owing him a reward. Those who are fully satisfied by this convenient naturalism are apparently content to ignore the theological self-contradiction which it involves: for how can man arrive at union with the transcendent and infinite God by his own powers? What proportion is there between the will and intelligence of man, and the love and truth of God? Can man bridge the gulf between the natural and the supernatural by merely standing on the edge of the abyss and wishing? It is like trying to fly across the Grand Canyon by standing there flapping your arms as if they were wings.

It is true that man can, by his natural powers, arrive at a natural and imperfect beatitude. This may include within itself a certain knowledge of God, even a kind of seemingly mystical contemplation. Those who are satisfied with the Pelagian solution find this to be quite enough for them. And if that is the case, we are quite willing to admit that they are right as far as they go. For they can, by their own power, reach what they think is the end of the journey. But what they call the end is not even the beginning.

* 26 *

WHATEVER may be the merits and nuances of all these different arguments, which have long ceased to be very interesting, they all have this in common: that they think there is fire to be stolen from the gods.

Summarizing all these false approaches, they all place man over against God. They set God and man in opposition to one another. They all assume basic, jealous hostility between man and God, a hostility which is centred on their respective rights, powers, and possessions. The assumption in all of them is that God is more or less resentful of man's natural powers, and above all of his freedom. This means that man must either save his soul by a Promethean *tour de force*, without God's help, or else that man must turn his freedom inside out, stew up all his natural gifts into a beautiful guilt-complex, and crawl towards God on his stomach to offer Him the results in propitiation.

What have these ideas to do with the love of God who "hates nothing that He has made" and who has sought man as His friend and His son—whose mercies are eternal and unchanging—who, though omnipotent, is incapable of taking back His love for man, His son, or changing it into hatred? All our strange ideas of conflict with God are born of the war that is within ourselves—the war between the "two laws"—the law of sin in our lower self and the law of God in our conscience. We are not fighting God, we are fighting ourselves. God, in His mercy, seeks to bring us peace—to reconcile us with ourselves. When we are reconciled to our true selves we find ourselves one with Him. "Who will deliver me from the body of this death? The grace of God through Jesus Christ our Lord." [Romans 7: 24, 25.] Grace is not a strange, magic substance which is subtly filtered into our souls to act as a kind of spiritual penicillin. Grace is unity, oneness within ourselves, oneness with God. Grace is the peace of friendship with God—and if it does not necessarily bring us a "felt" peace, it nevertheless gives us every reason to be at peace, if we could only understand and appreciate what it means. Grace means that *there is no opposition* between man and God, and that man is able to be sufficiently united within himself to live without opposition to God. Grace is friendship with God. And more —it is sonship. It makes us the "beloved sons" of God in whom He is "well pleased."

I<small>F</small> God made us intelligent and free, it was in order that
we might develop our freedom, extend our powers and
capacities of willing and loving to an unbelievable breadth,
and raise our minds to an unheard of vision of truth. But in
order that we might do all this (which is quite beyond our
natural powers) He Himself adds to our natural gifts the
gifts of grace which elevate and transfigure our nature,
healing its ills and expanding its powers, bringing forth into
actuality all its hidden resources in order to develop them
yet more by our mystical life in God. Is grace opposed to
nature? Not at all. It is opposed only to the *limitations*, to the
deficiencies, to the *weaknesses* of nature and to the infections
and illnesses nature has incurred through the misuse of its
own judgment and the abuse of its own freedom. Is grace
opposed to our own self-realization, to our perfection as
persons? Far from it. Grace is given us for the precise
purpose of enabling us to discover and actualize our deepest
and truest self. Unless we discover this deep self, which is
hidden with Christ in God, we will never really know
ourselves as persons. Nor will we know God. For it is by
the door of this deep self that we enter into the spiritual
knowledge of God. (And indeed, if we seek our true selves
it is not in order to contemplate ourselves, but to pass
beyond ourselves and find Him.) The "self" to which grace
is opposed is not merely the passionate, disordered, confused
self—the rambling and dishevelled "ego"—but much more
the tyrannical "super-ego," the rigid and deformed conscience which is our secret god and which with an infinitely
jealous resourcefulness defends its throne against the
coming of Christ.

* 28 *

THE Holy Spirit comes to set the whole house of our soul in order, to deliver our minds from immaturity, alienation fear and tenacious prejudice. If Christ is the Lamb of God Who takes away the sins of the world, then surely He sends His Spirit to deliver our souls from obsession with our feelings of guilt. This is the thing so many Christians refuse to see. They think Christ's power to deliver us from sin is not a real liberation but an assertion of His own rights over us. The truth is that it is both, for when God asserts "His rights" over us we become free. God is Truth and "the truth shall make you free."

This is precisely what we fail to understand. With respect to the higher freedom of grace, our natural freedom is simply a potency waiting to be developed. It is paradoxically by the grace of God that we finally achieve our full spiritual freedom and it is a gift of God that enables us to stand on our own feet.

* 29 *

HERE again we return to the Promethean tragedy and its inescapable dilemma. Prometheus does not want freedom as a gift. He wants to prove himself mature by the conquest of the jealous, secret fathers hidden in the clouds of Olympus. Therefore his life is a constant battle with the gods, and because it is a battle he cannot come to realize that true freedom is a state of peace with One he does not need to fight. Man is naturally mature and free when he has passed through all the stages of emotional and physical development that put him on the same level with other mature men, so that he is able to work together with them for the good of their community. Supernatural maturity raises us, in a certain sense, to a level of "equality" with God, a level on which we love Him as He loves us and cooperate with Him in the salvation of other men. *Dei adjutores sumus.* Christ, the Lamb of God who takes away the sins of the world, came to remove all obstacles to peace between ourselves and other men and God. He takes away not only the real sin which stands between us, but also the imaginary and illusory "sins" which go to make up our obsession with guilt and which often trouble us far more than our actual offences.

It is a strange thing that often our real sins are not "felt" in the emotions at all—and because they bring with them no strong sensation of shame, we can easily overlook them. And acts that are in no way seriously evil can cover us with confusion, making us feel as if we were criminals. The pain caused by these inoffensive actions is often so strong that we rebel against it completely. And in our rebellion, we imagine we have turned against God. After that, we dread to face Him, imagining that He wants to revenge Himself upon us. All this for nothing at all—for a social fault—something that momentarily made us look silly in the eyes of others. Surely, when we do this, we admit implicitly that we have no god but our own pride.

* 30 *

GRACE does not take hold of us as if we were planes or rockets guided by remote control. Yet there is a rather common tendency among spiritual men to imagine themselves as hollow, empty beings entirely governed and moved by a remote supernatural agency from outside and above themselves. This indeed pays homage to the idea that God is infinitely above man. But it entirely ignores the equally important truth of God's immanence within man. The spiritual man is not and cannot be a mere puppet, agitated from above by invisible wires which he himself does not perceive. If that were so, the spiritual life would be the worst kind of self-alienation. Sanctity would be nothing but schizophrenia.

In order to see the absurdity of such thoughts, we need only go back to St. Paul and read such words as these: "The charity of God is poured forth in our hearts by the Holy Spirit who has been given to us." [Romans 5: 5.] Not only is divine love in us, as the intimate principles of the highest kind of life, awareness, and activity, but the Spirit of God Himself dwells in us as the Gift of God, and He is there to be known and loved. He even desires His presence to be recognized in contemplative prayer. "But you shall know Him (the Spirit), because he will dwell with you, and be in you." [John 14: 17.]

* 31 *

THE scene in the Cenacle on Pentecost, when the Holy Spirit descended upon the Apostles in tongues of flame, is the final refutation of all Promethean theology. Here we see the full vindication of man in his longing for life. The life-instinct in man is the gift of a Living God who has brought us into existence in order that we may receive from Him the fullness of all life. He says to us "Which of you desires life, and takes delight in prosperous days?" [Psalm 33: 13] and the wisdom of grace is shown to us, in the Scriptures, as the source of life:

> Wisdom instructs her children
> and admonishes those who seek her.
> He who loves her loves life;
> those who seek her out win her favour.

He who holds her fast inherits glory
wherever he dwells, the Lord bestows blessings.

[Sirach 4: 11-13.]

The union of the Christian with God is the exact opposite of a Promethean exploit, because the Christian is not trying to steal something from God that God does not want him to have. On the contrary, he is striving with his whole heart to fulfil the will of God and lay hands upon that which God created him to receive. And what is that? It is nothing else but a participation in the life, and wisdom, and joy and peace of God Himself. This is greater than any other gift, higher than any other power. It is supreme freedom, the most perfect fulfilment. It has been called by the Fathers of the Church the *divinization* (*theosis*) of man. It is the ultimate in man's self-realization, for when it is perfected, man not only discovers his true self, but finds himself to be mystically one with the God by Whom he has been elevated and transformed.

The war between life and death within us is a war in which we are fighting not only for our life and our true freedom, but also, at the same time, for the glory and Kingdom of God. For when the truth of Christ has made us free, then we are what we are meant to be: images of the Divine Father, sons who work with the Father to establish His Kingdom of freedom.

IMAGE AND LIKENESS

IN the beginning, when the Lord created heaven and earth, the Spirit of God moved over the abyss. There was light. God divided light from darkness. He separated the waters. He called the firmament "heaven." He called the stars by their names, and they stood before Him, crying "We are here!" And they sang together before Him, as Job would hear them sing. There were seas, there was dry land. Seeds and grass sprang up out of the land. Dolphins played in the waters. Rare birds flew up out of the marshes between the land and the sea. Cries and clear songs filled all the forests, praised Him. Wild horses ran in their herds like wind upon the prairies. The glades gave up their deer as the leopard came down to the stream to quench her thirst. And where the lion looked up in the long brown grass a thousand antelopes raced down the bank of the great estuary with their beauty playing in the silent water.

The glory, the strength, the grace, the suppleness, the life of all things came into being at a command from God and praised Him. It was not because they praised Him that He looked at them: they praised Him beecause they were seen by Him. Their being, their life and their beauty existed because they were known by Him. Their very being, their reality, their existence, their movement, their life: these things praised Him because they were decided in His own wisdom and existed by an option of His liberty. He blessed them, therefore, in order that they might delight in their being, and in order that their existence should be beautiful and full of meaning in this world. By simply being, they would be able to say: "God knows us. God looks at us. He loves us and He has blessed us." Their being was their obedience to His option.

* 33 *

BUT when God made man, He did more than command him to exist. Adam, who was to be the son of God and God's helper in the work of governing the world He had created, was mysteriously formed by God, as the Old Testament so frequently tells us, as a potter forms a vessel out of clay. "Then the Lord God formed man out of the dust of the ground and breathed into his nostrils the breath of life, and man became a living being." [Genesis 2:7.]

The life of Adam, that is to say the "breath" which was to give actuality and existence and movement to the whole person of man, had mysteriously proceeded from the intimate depths of God's own life. Adam was created not merely as a living and moving animal who obeyed the command and will of God. He was created as a "son" of God because his life shared something of the reality of God's own breath or Spirit. For "breath" is the same as "spirit" (the Latin word *spiritus* is related to *spirare*, to breathe). The creation of Adam was not only a giving of life, but also a giving of love and of wisdom, so that at the very moment in which he came into being Adam was, by virtue of the supernatural and preternatural gifts which accompanied all his gifts of nature, in some sense "inspired." If the expression may be permitted, Adam's very existence was to be a kind of "inspiration." God intended not only to conserve and maintain Adam's bodily life. He would also foster and increase, even more directly and intimately, the spiritual life and activity which were the main reason for

Adam's existence. Adam, then, was meant from the very first to live and breathe in unison with God, for just as the soul was the life of Adam's body, so the Spirit of God, swelling in Adam, was to be the life of his soul. For him, then, to live would mean to "be inspired"—to see things as God saw them, to love them as He loved them, to be moved in all things ecstatically by the Spirit of God. And so for Adam ecstasy was by no means a violent interruption of the usual routine of life. There could be no violence, no alienation in such a life: in Paradise ecstasy is normal.

* 34 *

THE moment the first man sprang into being, moved by the breath of God, the depths of the centre of his perfect soul blazed with the silent, magnificent flame of Wisdom. Poised over the bright abyss of an interior purity that was perfectly serene because perfectly unconcerned with itself, Adam knew, before all else, that he possessed the truth, shining in the clean mirror of his own spirit. But more than that, he knew that his very spirit existed in and by and for the Truth. That Truth was more than a transcendental property of being. He saw himself in the Truth Who is a personal Absolute, the Lord of life and death, the Living God. He knew that he was himself real because he was loved by Him Who IS.

Who can comprehend or explain the mystery of what it means to awaken to one's own reality as an existential consequence of the fact that we are loved by Reality Itself? To see, in a contact too close for images or for concepts, and to understand in a vision too intimate to reach out to an object beyond itself, that our actuality is a spark in the infinite blaze of Pure Act Who is God. That our existence and being spring forth from the superabundant joy of His Existence. Above all, that we exist because He Who IS decrees, by an infinitely free option of His own liberality, that we should mirror analogously in ourselves His own Act of existing, and share His own liberty.

So at the first moment of his existence, Adam breathed the air of an infinitely pure freedom—a freedom which was poured into his soul directly by God in his creation. This supernatural self-determination made him capable of a freedom equal, in some sense, to the very freedom of God. It was a contingent freedom, that depended on his union with the Spirit who makes us all free. But apart from that one condition of *consenting* to perfect spiritual union, man's freedom was to be without limit. In the practically limitless horizons of this spiritual liberty which was, from the start, ingrained in Adam's very being by the free gift of God, Adam saw clearly that God was all and that nothing else mattered. All things were beautiful and good, but only when they were seen and loved in Him. All things were Adam's because Adam belonged to God—that is, belonged to Freedom. It was as if Truth, Love, Freedom, Power, Joy, Ecstasy had all been given to man to be his very being, his very nature. The superb transcendent actuality of these great gifts was, of course, all above man's nature. They were given to him to be his super-nature, for man, the child of God, was created to be in the highest sense a superman. He was to live, in fact, as a god.*

*The concept of a "superman" ought to be clear from what we have said on Promethean tendencies in religion. The Nietzschean concept of a superman is that of man who raises himself above himself by his own powers. It is simply the intensification of what is latent in his human nature. In the Biblical concept, man is raised above himself by supernatural gifts for which his nature has a passive and obediential potency, gifts by which these hidden potentialities receive a supereminent realization.

* 35 *

THE whole being of Adam, body and soul, heart, mind and spirit, passion and intelligence gathered up in the purity of a contemplation that was at the same time effortless and supreme, sang to God with the realization that he was full of God and thus became aware of himself and of the world as God's paradise. The great saint, Adam, the first man, Adam who was to be our father, was too strong and too clean to be inebriated by the wisdom in which his soul was swimming. But with the serenity and the happiness and the unconcern of his condition, the first child of God accepted the fullness of his reality in God, and looked into the existential presence (the "Face") of his Creator, and was happy.

The lowest in the order of spiritual beings, and the highest of those that had a place in material creation, Adam, containing in himself the whole human race, was placed at the metaphysical cross-roads of a universe that was charged with vision, love and spiritual experience.

* 36 *

IF, among spirits, the spirit of man was the least glorious, perhaps it was also, for that very reason, the most cherished and the most favoured by the love of God. For in sharing His light with the least of His spiritual creatures God was giving a more evident manifestation of His own liberality and love. And if, among bodily things, man was the most exalted, it was in order that he might contemplate God and praise Him as the high priest of the universe. Placed at the exact ontological centre of creation, a little less than the angels but charged with command over brute and inanimate beings, Adam was the anointed mediator between God and His world, the priest who offered all things to God without destroying them or harming them. For destruction did not enter the concept of sacrifice until after the fall. It was in the mystical union of Adam's soul with God that the whole world was offered and consecrated to God in sacrifice. It was in the sounding solitude of Adam's understanding that things without reason became able to adore their Creator, in the flaming silence of Adam's wisdom all that existed and breathed and grew and ran and multiplied upon the earth was united with God in worship and in communion. The intellect and the freedom of Adam, transfigured by the presence of the Creating and Sanctifying Spirit of the Lord, were the temple in which all the material world justified its existence by being raised to the level of intelligibility and value. The world was, by the very presence of God in it, wonderful and sacred. But the sacred character of the world needed a witness and an interpreter. This was the function of the contemplative and active Adam, appointed to "dress the garden of Paradise and to keep it." By his morning and evening knowledge of God, Adam would know the Lord not only in contemplation but in action—not only in his own soul but in material creation. Everywhere he looked, Adam was beset by light, and wonder, and understanding.

This, in the plan of God, was to have been our own condition.

* 37 *

WHERE the second creation narrative, in Genesis, shows God forming Adam as a potter shapes his clay, and breathing into his mouth the breath of life, the first narrative is less anthropomorphic, more speculative. In much more mysterious language, God (Elohim) says: "Let us make mankind in our image and likeness." [Genesis 1: 26.] The Fathers of the Church, meditating on these lines, interpreted them in various manners. Some preferred to see the "divine image" in man's command over the rest of creation. Man resembles God in so far as he too, like God, is a worker, a ruler, a creator and a father. His creativity, inseparable from his nature, is the "image." The "likeness"—in which the image is perfected by a completely faithful correspondence to its original, would then be man's actual use of his powers as a creator, worker and father, as God Himself would use them. Man becomes an effective instrument and imitator of his divine Father in governing the world. He makes, for himself, a new world within the world God has made. He constructs a "city"—a society—which is a microcosm perfectly reflecting the order established by God, a living, organic whole in which the creatures of God, elevated above their original destiny by productive use in all the arts by which man lives, praise God now no longer in themselves but with man, in his society. Thus society itself becomes an extension of the sanctified spirit of man, a temple into which all creation enters in order to give praise to God.

This theory conceives man as oriented towards an active life in the world. He is a "doer," a "maker," who praises God with the work of his hands and of his intelligence. And in the line of this thought, original sin would be a perversion of man's active instincts, a turning of man's creativity away from God so that he produces and creates not the society and the temple which God's own creation demands as its fulfilment, but a temple of man's own power. The world is then exploited for the glory of man, not for the glory of God. Man's power becomes an end in itself. Things are not merely used, they are wasted, destroyed. Men are no longer workers and "creators" but tools of production, instruments for profit. The ultimate extreme of this process of degeneration is reached when all man's powers are directed to spoilage, rapine and destruction, and when his society is geared not only against God, but against the most fundamental natural interests of man himself.

* 38 *

OTHER interpreters of Genesis prefer to think that the divine image in man is in the orientation of his spirit toward contemplative union with God. Man resembles God in so far as he is a contemplative. This means that man is not only pre-eminently a thinker, but a "seer," a prophet who gazes into the deep things of God and gives utterance to what he sees. He is a man of prayer, a man of the spirit. And this characteristic is found, by some of the Fathers, in the very structure of man's soul.

St. Augustine seeks God in the most intimate depths of his own spirit. At the summit of his own self-realization, which he calls the *memoria*, Augustine finds not only himself but the light by which he sees himself as he really is. And in this light, he is aware of God from whom the light comes. His awareness of God instantly broadens out into love. Charity springs up in the illumination of his soul's depths and carries him out of himself and beyond himself to the God who is enthroned in the very summit of his own personal being: the *apex mentis* or the "spark" of the soul.

* 39 *

THE "image" of God is found in the soul's structure—awareness, thought, love. But the "likeness" of God is effected in the soul when these powers receive their own fulfilment and super-actualization in a spiritual experience of Him Whose image they are. When the awareness or "*memoria*" becomes consciousness of God, when the intelligence is enlightened in a spiritual understanding of God and when the will raises the whole soul above itself in an ecstasy of love for God, then the "image" is perfected in likeness. In order to understand better the relation of "image" and "likeness" let us consider a comparison. A blurred photograph of a person is a picture or an image of the person, but it is overexposed or double-exposed or otherwise defective. A clear photograph is not only a picture of the person but is a "likeness" of the person, giving an exact idea of him. And so St. Augustine says: "In this image (which is the soul) *the resemblance of* God will be perfect when the vision of God is perfect." [*De Trinitate* XIV, C.15, n. 23.]

This doctrine is implied in St. John, who writes: "Beloved, now we are the children of God (image), and it has not yet appeared what we shall be. We know that, when he appears, we shall be like to him (likeness), for we shall see him just as he is." [I John 3 : 2.] This presupposes a theory of knowledge which demands that the intelligence be conformed to its object or notionally identified with it. Here however it is a question not only of a notional identification but of a union of the whole soul and the whole person with God. This is the end for which we were created in God's image.

* 40 *

THE Fathers of the Church make other distinctions between the image and likeness. Some say that the image is in our nature and that the likeness is imparted by grace. Others distinguished between the *imago creationis*, the image of God that was actually in Adam, who was created with all the gifts of nature and of grace at the same time, and the *imago recreationis* which comes into being in the man who is baptized and sanctified by the presence of the divine Spirit. The Fathers commonly recognize that the image of God in the soul is the "seat" of God's presence in the soul—a throne which can, unfortunately, remain empty. For although God is always present in all things by His power, knowledge and being, He is said to be "absent" from the spiritual beings in whom His presence is not at least implicitly acknowledged or desired. Some of the Fathers stress the idea that "the true image of God is the man who does good." [Clement of Alexandria, *Stromata*, 2: 19.] (Cf. Origen, *Homilia in Leviticum*, 4: 3, "If you are merciful, the image of God is in you.") Others, like St. Gregory of Nyssa, who in this respect influenced St. Bernard, are absorbed in the thought that the divine image in man is especially constituted by man's freedom.

* 41 *

To resume all these ideas, the image of God is the summit of spiritual consciousness in man. It is his highest peak of self-realization. This is achieved not merely by reflection on his actual, present self: one's actual self may be far from "real," since it may be profoundly alienated from one's own deep spiritual identity. To reach one's "real self" one must, in fact, be delivered by grace, virtue and asceticism, from that illusory and false "self" whom we have created by our habits of selfishness and by our constant flights from reality. In order to find God, Whom we can only find in and through the depths of our own soul, we must therefore first find ourselves. To use common figures of speech, we must "return to ourselves," we must "come to ourselves." Our ordinary life, cluttered and obstructed as it is by our own bad habits of thought and action as well as by the bad habits of the society we live in, is little more than a semi-conscious, torpid kind of existence when it is compared with the real life of our deep selves—the life that we are all supposed to be leading. To awaken to the realities of the spirit and to discover the image of God within us is therefore something quite different from a Platonic awakening to the spirituality of our formal human essence as distinguished from the concrete materiality that weighs us down. The Christian view does not make an abstract division between matter and spirit. It plunges into the existential depths of the concrete union of body and soul which makes up the human person, and by clearing the spiritual temple of all those ways of thinking which obstruct our inward vision, opens the way to an existential communion at the same time with ourselves and with God in the actual, subsisting, spiritual reality of our own inviolable being. In this way, the body is not discarded (which is in any case not possible) but elevated and spiritualized. Man is not cut in half, he is drawn together and finds himself more of one piece, more integrated than ever before.

* 42 *

FINALLY, let us pause a moment to consider the meaning of the word "spirit" that we have been using. In St. Paul, who sets the tone for all patristic thought on this particular point as in so many others, the "spirit" or "*pneuma*" is distinct from the "soul" (*psyche*) and even from the intelligence (*nous*):

For the word of God is living and efficient . . . and extending even to the division of soul and spirit. [Hebrews 4: 12.]

45

St. Thomas, commenting on this passage, while conceding that St. Paul adopts the Platonic division of man into body, soul and spirit, denies a real distinction between the soul (life principle) and spirit (principle of understanding and freedom). He says:

> The essence of the soul is one and the same, and by its essence the soul gives life to the body, while by its power, which is called the intelligence, it is the principle of understanding. And by this power it understands eternal things. [*Lectio 2 in Caput IV Epistolae ad Hebraeos.*]

First of all the spirit means simply the highest spiritual faculty in man—the intelligence, as a principle either of speculative or of practical understanding. In other words, the spirit is the summit of man's nature and the source from which his most personal and characteristic and elevated activities are derived. The Apostle uses the word in this sense when he says: "For who among men knows the things of a man save the spirit of the man which is in him?" [I Corinthians 2: 11.]

The context of this last quotation introduces us immediately to the second meaning of the word "spirit". This is the one to which we must pay the strictest attention. The "mystic" is simply the "spiritual" man in the fullest sense of the word "spiritual" (*pneumatikos*). Here the *pneuma* is still man's natural faculty, it is still the summit of man's nature. But that summit has been transformed. Though remaining essentially the same, it has acquired an entirely new and different modality by the fact that the Spirit of God is present within it. The *pneuma* is then not only man's spirit alone, but man's spirit united with the Spirit of God. It is the deified or transfigured spirit of man, justified by faith and activated by divine grace, living a life of charity. The actions of this *pneuma* are strictly our own, and yet at the same time they belong to God. When a man prays "in the spirit" it is he who prays indeed, but it is also the Spirit of God who prays in him, guiding him and showing how to commune with God beyond language and understanding. The *pneuma* is the spirit of man moved and directed by the Spirit of God, liberated by deep faith and illumined by the wisdom of God Himself.

* 43 *

THOUGH the word *pneuma* means now the spirit of man without God, and now the Spirit of God without man, the most important meaning of the word is that in which the spirit of man is shown in the most intimate possible union with the Spirit of God so that the two are in all truth "one spirit." "But he who cleaves to the Lord is one spirit with him." [I Corinthians 6: 17.]

It is in this particular sense that, throughout these meditations, we speak of man "finding himself in God." Man does not fully know himself so long as he is isolated in his own individual self-hood. His identity comes to light only when it fully confronts the "other." We are created for freedom, for the options and self-dedications implied by the highest kind of love. We discover and develop our freedom precisely by making those decisions which take us out of ourselves to meet others as they really are. But we are incapable of knowing and experiencing reality adequately unless we see things in the light of Him who is All Being, all real. The Spirit of God, penetrating and enlightening our own spirit from within ourselves, teaches us the ways of a freedom by which alone we enter into vital spiritual contact with these around us. In this contact we become aware of our own autonomy, our own identification. We find out who we really are. And having made the discovery we are ready for the love and service of others.

PART II

FREE SPEECH (*Parrhesia*)

* 44 *

THE Patristic doctrine of man's creation in the image and likeness of God proclaims that the creation was indeed a triumph of life. When God breathed into the face of Adam, everything in man came alive: not only his body, not only his mind, but also his spirit in which the image of God was hidden. And the image of God was alive with likeness to God, that is to say with contemplation. The spirit of Adam lived by the life and the wisdom and the knowledge and the love of his Creator and Sanctifier. God lived in him and he lived in God. The closeness of this union has become clear to us in our consideration of the Pauline concept of the *pneuma*.

* 45 *

WHEN we say that the creation of the first son of God was a triumph of life, we mean that every aspect of human living was exalted and sanctified at the dawn of man's history. Man's whole existence, not only in his relations with God but in his relations with his own kind (Eve) and with the rest of the created world, were transfigured by divine insights and by an awareness of the inmost reality and value of everything that had come from the hand of God. Adam was not only a contemplative but, as we have seen, a man of action. For we can combine both theories of the divine image into one, and say with both Patristic schools that Adam is at the same time a seer and a maker, a prophet and a king, a father and a husbandman. In him the lives of contemplation and action combine, as they were always meant to do, in a perfect harmony made possible by the fact that contemplation preserves its just rights to primacy by the life where God remains always enthroned, in a transforming and unifying light, at the summit of the human spirit.

* 46 *

THE concept of man's intimacy with God in work as well as in contemplation was sometimes rendered by the Fathers in the Greek word *parrhesia* for which perhaps the most convenient translation is "free speech." The word represents, in fact, the rights and privileges of a citizen in a Greek city state. This "free speech" is at once the duty and the honour of speaking one's own mind fully and frankly in the civil assemblies by which the state is governed. The Genesis story tells us of Adam's "freedom of speech" with God not so much by directly describing it as by saying what replaced it when it was taken away. The *parrhesia* of Adam in Eden is known by inference, by implication. We see it by the contrast of his state after the fall with what is implied to have gone before.

This is clear in the conversation with God that follows "the fall." We shall return later to the scene in which Adam and Eve are ashamed of their nakedness and make themselves "aprons" to conceal themselves from God. This was the first step in that self-alienation which resulted from man's refusal to accept himself as he actually is—a refusal which constitutes the very essence of original sin.

When they heard the sound of the Lord God walking in the garden in the cool of the day, the man and his wife hid themselves from the Lord God among the trees of the garden. But the Lord God called the man and said to him: "Where are you?" And he said: "I heard You in the garden, and I was afraid because I was naked, and I hid."

Then He said: "Who told you that you were naked? You have eaten then of the tree of which I commanded you not to eat." [Genesis 3: 8-11.]

Before the fall Adam, the prince of creation, conversed familiarly with God in the sense that he was constantly meeting Him in flashes of mystical intuition either in the existential reality of his own spiritual depths or in the reality of objective creation. He walked the earth, therefore, as one who had no master under God. He could be conscious of his own autonomy, under God, as the priest and king of all that God had made. Knowing no rebellion in the simplicity and order of his own being, he was also obeyed by all creatures. His mind had a perfect knowledge of himself and of the world around him and his will acted in perfect accordance with his vision of truth. This supreme harmony of all his powers flowed from their unity at the summit of Adam's own being, in the *pneuma*, which was one with God.

* 47 *

THE image of *parrhesia* which suggests to us Adam conversing familiarly with a God Who came down to walk in the afternoon in the garden of Paradise is strangely effective in bringing home to us the spiritual implications of Adam's oneness with himself, with God, and with the world around him. The "free speech" the Fathers speak of is a symbolic expression of that perfect adaptation to reality, which came from the fact that man was exactly what he was intended to be by God: that is to say, he was perfectly himself. To be perfectly oneself, in the highest mystical sense in which we are constantly using this expression in these pages, not only gave man access to all the latent powers of his own rich human nature, not only placed him in complete communication with all created things by giving him command over them, but finally kept him in constant and unimpeded contact with the Spirit of God.

But if the metaphor of *parrhesia* expresses man's perfect actualization by his supernatural union with the Spirit of God, then at the same time it expresses the union and cohesion of all the natural, preternatural and supernatural gifts which made man what God intended him to be. *Parrhesia* then symbolizes the perfect communication of man's intelligence with God by knowledge (*gnosis*) and contemplation (*theoria*). It symbolizes also the perfect communion of his will with God by charity. Adam's senses and his passions were in perfect subjection to his intelligence and will and these, in their turn, were perfectly united to the Spirit of God.

* 48 *

As St. Thomas* points out, the fact that Adam's intelligence was perfectly united to God caused his lower powers to be perfectly subjected to his intelligence. And this, in turn, brought about the perfect subjection of the body to the soul. In a word, one of the most significant results of Adam's spiritual union with God was the fact that it completely spiritualized and divinized not only his spirit but also his body. Consequently his body could not be separated from his soul, as long as his soul was not separated from God. Immortality was the direct result of Adam's *parrhesia*, and it was one of the most eloquent expressions of his "citizen-

---

Summa Theologica, I, Q. 95, a.1. Cf. Dom Anselme Stolz, O.S.B., *Théologie de la Mystique*, Chevetogne, 1947, p. 114.

ship" among the spiritual beings who serve God in heaven. But at the same time the death of the body, by its separation from the soul, was simply the outward manifestation of the separation of the soul from God, the true and spiritual death which Adam died when he sinned.

* 49 *

Parrhesia was the free spiritual communication of being with Being, Adam's existential communion with the reality around him in and through the Reality of God which he constantly experienced within himself. It derived all its power and meaning from the union of his soul with God in "one spirit." From this union flowed the gifts of supernatural wisdom, contemplation and science, the tranquillity of an impassible nature, a nature that could not die as long as union subsisted. Life reigned in Adam as long as the truth made him free from error, ignorance, suffering, confusion, disorder and death. But in order for the truth to reign in his soul, Adam had to consent constantly to the illumination of God's light within him. He had to consent to see himself and all things in that pure light and in no other. He remained in contact with God, with himself, and with the reality around him as long as he permitted no lie to come between himself and the light. And his intelligence, which until then could not be deceived, simply admitted the darkness and turned away from light under a command from his free will, which remained capable of rejecting the truth. Adam's fall was therefore the wilful acceptance of unreality, the consent to receive and even prefer a lie to the truth about himself and about his relationship to God. This lie robbed him of the innocence by which he saw nothing but good in himself, in things and in God and endowed him with the power to know evil, not only speculatively but by experience. The experience of falsity destroyed in him the instinctive taste for spiritual truth. Illusion entered in to spoil the existential flow of communication between his soul and God. *Parrhesia* was at an end not because God no longer consented to speak with Adam, but because Adam, stripped of his sincerity, ashamed to be what in fact he was, determined to fly from God and from reality, which he could no longer face without a disguise.

* 50 *

ALTHOUGH Adam was first of all a contemplative, Genesis seems to place all the stress on his *active life* in Paradise. In Paradise there was no opposition between action and contemplation. We too, if we recover, in Christ, the paradisiacal life of Adam which He has restored to us, are supposed to discover that the opposition between them vanishes at last. Therefore it is interesting to consider Adam at work in the Garden of Eden, and find out that even his activity had an essentially contemplative character, since it was entirely impregnated with light and significance by his union with God.

"The Lord God," says Genesis [2: 15], "took the man and placed him in the garden of Eden to till it and to keep it." The sentence is as deeply mysterious as any other in this wonderful text. In the first place we might expect it to have a spiritual sense, in which the meaning would be that Adam's main task would be to preserve his own union with God, his own perfect and original contact with all reality in its source. However, the Fathers also interpret it literally, since from the start man was to act as God's instrument in cultivating and developing the natural creation.

FREE SPEECH

St. Augustine, who seems to have been very fond of farming and gardening and of all the forms of manual labour traditionally assigned to monks, is quick to point out that if Adam worked even in Paradise, work is by no means to be regarded by us as an evil. Nor is it, by its nature, a penance for sin. He proves this from the nature of the work itself. Even in our fallen state, when the earth brings forth "thorns and thistles," there are, says Augustine, "some men who find gardening such a delight that it is for them a great penalty to be called away from it to any other occupation."*

Adam's whole attitude about work was disinterested. He did not need to work in order to live but he worked because "his soul desired it" (says St. Augustine in the same text). His reason for working was that in using a power God had given him, and in serving God by his own intelligence and skill, he praised God more perfectly and by that very fact raised his own existence to a higher level of reality and of value. Adam's work was an important aspect of his existential communion with the reality of nature and of the supernatural by which he was surrounded. It was a conversation with God, a moment of Adam's *parrhesia*. Here are some of the phrases with which St. Augustine described it.†

Whatever may be now the delights of gardening, in those days (in Eden) its delights were far greater, when there was nothing that constituted an obstacle, either from heaven or from earth. There was then no affliction in labour but exhilaration for the will, when all the things created by God, helped by man's work brought forth richer and more abundant fruits. . . . Hence the Creator was more abundantly praised since He had given

*De Genesi ad Litteram, viii, 8. (The quotes from Augustine that immediately follow are all from this text.)
†Vide supra.

to the rational soul, placed in an animal body, the ability to work and the power to work as much as his soul desired, rather than the need to work, against his will, as much as his body demanded.

The key to this whole conception is found in the spiritual liberty enjoyed by Adam, in the tranquillity of soul which made him able to work "as much as his soul desired." The word desire, here, is free from the tyranny of passion.

The work men do because they are driven by ambition or love of money is quite another thing. They may "like" it, but it is nevertheless a slavery. Its orientation is exactly the opposite to the one we are considering here. Adam's work was worship. The work of those who work because they are driven by passion or cupidity is not worship but struggle, not freedom but (psychologically) compulsion. If our work is to become contemplative, we must be free enough from things to be able to respect them instead of merely exploiting them. We must not only use them, but value their use, and appreciate them justly for what they really are. We must understand what we are doing, and we must be able to measure and control the effects of our actions not only on the things and persons immediately concerned, but also on others connected with them. We must work with a sense of responsibility towards living and growing things and towards the men we live with. We must work with some consciousness of the value of human society, which is the beneficiary of our labours. In a word, our work ought to be a dialogue with reality, and therefore a conversation with God. This, however, it cannot be unless it is first of all carried out with some measure of intelligence, with humility, and above all with some awareness of the laws of cause and effect and some attention to the remote consequences of our actions.

The idea of work as a dialogue with reality and with God is beautifully expressed by St. Augustine, who says:

What greater or more wonderful spectacle is there, or where can human reason better enter into a dialogue with the nature of things, than when seeds have been planted, shoots laid out, shrubs transplanted, grafts inserted. It is as though one were questioning each root and seed, asking it what it can do and what it cannot do; whence it derives the power to do it, or why it cannot do it; what help it receives from its own interior power, and what from exterior help and diligence. And in this dialogue we come to understand how neither he who plants nor he who waters is anything, but God who giveth the increase. For that work which is applied exteriorly is fruitful only by the action of Him who created and ruled and ordered all from within.

Augustine infers here that Adam acquired scientific knowledge by experiment, but he also possessed an infused or mystical science (*gnosis*) which appears in the scene where he names all the animals. The mysterious and primitive beauty of the text, with its anthropomorphic images, tells us better than anything of the union of Adam's mind with God: "When the Lord God had formed out of the ground all the beasts of the field and the birds of the air, He brought them to the man to see what he would call them: for that which the man called each of them would be its name." [Genesis 2: 19.]

In a humorous and deeply existential poem, Mark Van Doren has remarked on the fact that the animals are not at all conscious of having been named and classified by men.

> What names? They have not heard the sound,
> Nor in their silence thought the thing.
> They are not notified they live,
> Nor ask who set them wandering.

The poet goes on to remind us that the animals "simply

are" and he comments that if they spoke they would tell
us that the same is true of ourselves. The information might
prove so disconcerting that our objectivized knowledge of
ourselves would collapse along with everything else in the
"end" of our intentional world.

> Simply they are. And so with us;
> And they would say it if they spoke;
> And we might listen, and the world
> Be uncreated at one stroke.

The intuition in the last line is deeper than the humour
seems to indicate. It is, in fact, quite true that Adam's
naming of the animals was a second creation, a noumenal, an
intentional creation of them, giving them an objective,
communicable existence in the minds of men.

* 52 *

ONE of the most significant acts of that *parrhesia* we have
been describing is this one in which God initiates Adam into
the very mystery of creative action. But how? Not by doing
violence to his human nature, intelligence and freedom and
using him as an agent in drawing something out of nothing.
On the contrary, Adam's function is to *look* at creation, see
it, recognize it, and thus give it a new and spiritual existence
within himself. He imitates and reproduces the creative
action of God first of all by repeating, within the silence of
his own intelligence, the creative word by which God
made each living thing. The most interesting point in the
story is the freedom left to Adam in this work of "creation."
The name is decided, chosen, not by God but by Adam.
"For that which the man called each of them, *would be its
name*." It is as if the Lord waited upon Adam to confer this
accidental perfection upon His created world—as if there

were one final touch that was left entirely to man's freedom, God had decreed what each thing should be, and He had left its being in the sanctuary of His own divine silence. It was for Adam to draw each being notionally out of the silence and hold it up to the light of his own intelligence, coining the brand new word that would signify the correspondence between the *thought* in the mind of Adam and the *reality* in the mind of God. Thus Adam's science was a discovery not only of names but of *essences*.

* 53 *

ADAM'S contemplative life, which had begun with a recognition of himself in God and of God in himself, and which would expand into a dialogue between Adam and God through creation, now reaches a new level in which man not only learns how to look at things and see them for what they are, but acquires means of conveying his idea of them to others. Here begins the dialogue with other men.

After having drawn forth the living beings out of nothingness, God elicits from the depths of Adam's own liberty words, names and signs. These, in their turn, will flower into many kinds of creative intellectual activity. They will become, first of all, poems which will express man's inexpressible intuitions of the hidden reality of created things. They will become philosophy and science, by which man will objectify and universalize his private vision of the world into thought-systems that can be shared by everyone. Finally words will become *sacred* signs. They will acquire the power to set apart certain elements of creation and make them holy. By "the word of God and prayer" every creature of God, good in itself, can be sanctified [I Timothy 4: 5]. That is to say that besides being in their very nature signs of

God their Creator, creatures can become, at the word of man, *sacred* signs and even sacraments. They can acquire the power not only to manifest the might and being of God by their own existence and their qualities, but they can above all be signs of the infinite transcendence of Him Who is Holy, and they can be symbols of the hidden immanent action of the Holy One in His created universe.

This is a matter of the greatest importance. The language and the thought of man need to rise above the level of distinct concepts which, though they may give us accurate information, fall short of the existential mystery of the things they represent. How much more do they fail to plumb the abyss of infinite actuality in the Being of God? Yet when they renounce their aspiration to circumscribe all they signify within clear and definite limits, words can still travel, and take us with them, into the mystery of God and into the sanctuary of Him who is Holy. They can manifest something of His presence within us and, more than that, they can even cause Him to be present within us in that special light which is the virtue of faith. "Faith then depends on hearing, and hearing on the word of Christ." [Romans 10: 17.]

* 54 *

THROUGH the words of man, charged by a divine gift with the mysterious sanctifying power that belongs to the Holy One alone, holiness can become a visible and tangible thing. Sensible and material realities can become matter of sacraments as well as other signs of the union of man with God (sacramentals). The rites and liturgy of man acquire the power to evoke the divine mystery that eye has not seen, that ear has not heard and that it has not entered into the heart of man to conceive. Words, therefore, become seeds of prayer and of contemplation, instruments of man's transfiguration into the likeness of the Holy God Whom no one can see without dying. Words and symbols lie in the depths of man's inherited store of knowledge and memory and even in the souls of men who have completely forgotten God these archetypal seeds of divinity and mystery still lie hidden, waiting to germinate like the grains of wheat laid away thousands of years ago, with a Pharaoh under his pyramid.

* 55 *

THE personal and direct grasp of sacred realities by each individual soul is an incommunicable experience. The mystical vision of God cannot be passed on from father to son. But the aptitude for that vision may be inherited. The capacity to sense the holiness of God in His creation, and to respond to Him with worship, more or less, is always there. It needs to be brought to life by the proper signs and symbols. But the capacity of signs and symbols to fruitfully affect the souls of men is, again, circumscribed by a greater or less sensitivity to symbolism. This sensitivity may always virtually be there, but its actuality is something that is all too easily lost, though not too hard to acquire. Sensitivity to religious symbolism has never been so dead as in our time even, and perhaps especially, among religious men.

* 56 *

WORDS lose their capacity to convey the reality of holiness in proportion as men focus on the symbol rather than on what it symbolizes. The sense of the sacred, of the "numinous" without which there can hardly be any real or living religion, depends entirely on our ability to transcend our own human signs, to penetrate them and pass beyond their manifest intelligibility into the darkness of mystery, to grasp the reality they can suggest but never fully contain. The mere repetition of consecrated formulas is not, therefore, holiness itself. But words are the only normal keys by which we can unlock, for one another, the doors of the sanctuary and direct one another in to the Holy of Holies where each of us must enter the sacred darkness in love and in fear, to find the Lord alone.

* 57 *

ADAM had named the animals before he had anyone to talk to. This suggests that words are considered, by the authors of Genesis, to have a function other than that of simple communication—and it would seem that this other function is primary. Adam names the animals, not for their benefit, not for the benefit of any other human being, not merely even for his own. But words are drawn forth from his soul by God because there is an absolute value in words as the witnesses of essences that are stable and eternal. The primary function of the word is a contemplative rather than a communicative statement of what exists. Even if we never talk to anyone, or think in terms of conversations with others, the mental word dressed in its proper sound stands in the depths of our intelligence to bear witness to reality and to worship God. In this sense the word is a kind of seal upon our intellectual communion with Him, before it becomes a means of communication with other men.

* 58 *

THE creation of Eve from the side of Adam brings us to

another level of mystery and contemplation. In the creation of human society we have at once the symbol and type of the perfect society, the Church, the union of mankind with God in Christ, which is "the Mystery" *par excellence.*

Adam first realized his existential communion with God when he awoke from nothingness in the first moment of his existence to find himself created in the image and likeness of God. He awoke to the reality of God in living things when he became aware of his mission as a worker in God's creation. He learned to see and understand other sentient beings and he discovered another means of communion with the hidden holiness of God when he created language. Now he awakens to a most perfect form of existential communion in human love.

The Lord "cast a deep sleep" upon Adam, took out one of his ribs and built flesh around it and made it into a woman, since it was not good for man to be alone. Adam awoke, and once again proved that for him the primary function of language was to bear witness to the hidden meaning of things rather than to "talk about" them. Adam was no pragmatist, and so, he did not begin by conversing with woman, as soon as she was made, but he uttered a gnomic poem at once to himself and to the whole universe: "Then the man said, She now is bone of my bone, and flesh of my flesh; she shall be called Woman, for from man she has been taken. For this reason a man leaves his father and mother, and clings to his wife, and the two become one flesh." [Genesis 2: 23, 24.]

The mystery that had taken place in his ecstasy was the mystery of a solitude that became society—the mystery of the person finding himself reproduced and completed in one who is "the same" and yet "another." Adam, perfectly whole and isolated in himself, as a person, needs nevertheless to find himself perfected, without division or diminution, by the gift of himself to another. He needs to give himself in order to gain himself. The law of self-renunciation is not merely a consequence of sin, for charity is the fundamental rule of the whole moral universe. Without it, man will always be less than himself since without it he will always be imprisoned within himself. He will be less than a man. In order to be fully himself, man needs to love another as himself. In order to realize himself, man has to risk the diminution and even the total loss of all his reality, in favour of another, for if any man would save his life he must lose it. We are never fully ourselves until we realize that those we truly love become our "other selves." Seeing this, we are capable of beginning to grasp that God also loves us as He loves Himself. Without this awareness, there can be no perfect communion.

* 59 *

IN the mystery of social love there is found the realization of "the other" not only as one to be loved by us, so that we may perfect ourselves, but also as one who can become more perfect by loving us. The vocation to charity is a call not only to love but to *be loved*. The man who does not care at all whether or not he is loved is ultimately unconcerned about the true welfare of the other and of society. Hence we cannot love unless we also consent to be loved in return.

The life of "the other" is not only a supplement, an adjunct to our own. Our companion is our helper, and it is in helping one another that we give glory to God. What is seen singly and indivisibly in His one Nature and Three Persons, should be seen refracted and multiplied in the many subsisting natures of men united with one another in society. That it is not seen so is due to the fact that all mankind fell and was shattered with Adam, and the pieces of the great broken image that was meant to mirror God in man's society can only be brought together again in Him who is our peace, bringing the divided fragments into unity.

We are one in the new Adam: Christ.

> But now in Christ Jesus you, who were once afar off, have been brought near through the blood of Christ. For he himself is our peace, he it is who has made both one, and has broken down the intervening wall of the enclosure, the enmity, in his flesh. [Ephesians 2: 13, 14.]

But in Eve Adam recognizes not only the companion but the bride. The union of two in one flesh is not chiefly for consolation and mutual support. It is above all creative and fecund. It is not only a contemplative recognition of life, but an active production of life: not only a knowing of life but a giving of it, a sharing and communication which elevates marriage to that sublime spiritual level in which action and contemplation are capable of fusion in the brilliant darkness of mystery.

* 60 *

IN the union of man and woman it is no longer words that are symbols of the mystery of God's holiness, but persons. God appears in them as sacred, not only in the sense that life itself seems sacred to us, because it is mysterious, but in the sense that the productive union of those who are humanly in love with each other is a sacred symbol of the infinite giving and diffusion of goodness which is the inner law of God's own life. Yet since the sacredness of God is precisely His transcendence, the marriage of human beings is a sacred symbol in this other sense: it reminds us of the fact that in the kingdom of heaven they "neither marry nor be given in marriage." [Mark 12: 25.]

Above all, in this eloquent mystery of marriage, as St. Paul tells us, Adam saw something of the union of Christ and the Church. [Ephesians 5: 32.] The most exalted manifestation of God's holiness is not to be found in the flaming theophanies of the Old Testament but in the charity of Christ towards men. The married love that is transfigured by the Church's sacrament reproduces something of this love by which Christ sanctified His Church, and the natural mystery of the communication of life by love becomes a supernatural mystery of the communication of holiness by charity. The bodily and spiritual love which becomes the source of physical life is at once selfish and unselfish. The spiritual love which is the wellspring of holiness is entirely unselfish and entirely sacred. The fertility of physical love is necessary in the sense that it obeys a blind demand of natural instinct. The fecundity of spiritual love is always perfectly free, and its freedom is proportionate to its unselfishness. It asks nothing merely for itself, except the freedom and the ability to give. Already, in the woman he saw before him, and in the love that united him to her, Adam also saw the charity and the self-sacrifice that would enable human beings to love one another spiritually and live as one body in Christ.

* 61 *

EVEN though in his union with Eve Adam recognized the marriage of divinity and humanity in Christ, he probably did not foresee what was to be the deepest aspect of *parrhesia* —one which could never have been revealed without his

66

own sin. It is a marvellous thing indeed for innocent Adam
to approach God with confidence and speak to the Holy
One (without forgetting His transcendent holiness) as to a
Father and in some sense as to an equal (for He has called us
His friends, and there is no true friendship except between
equals). But *parrhesia* is a far more marvellous thing in men
who are sinners, who are forced to recognize themselves as
burdened with guilt, men who have offended God and
have fled from the sight of Him because they preferred their
own illusions to His truth. It is a great paradox that God
comes on earth not to seek the company of the just but the
company of sinners. For when the Lord comes into the world
as a Saviour, the men with whom He seeks to talk familiarly,
because He loves them and wants to make them His
friends, are precisely the sinners.

To recognize this truth is to recognize at the same time
that no man, whether good or bad, can lay claim in strict
justice to the love of God, because love is not like that. It
has to be given as a free gift, or not at all. The sinner who is
ready to accept love as a gift from God is far closer to God
than the "just" man who insists on being loved for his own
merits. For the former will soon stop sinning (since he will
be loved by God), and the latter has probably already begun
to sin.

How wise is the Church when she sings of Adam's
"happy fault"—*felix culpa*. We remember the question
Jesus asked of Simon the leper: "A certain money-lender
had two debtors; the one owed five hundred denarii, the
other fifty. As they had no means of paying, he forgave
them both. Which of them, therefore, will love him more?"
[Luke 7: 41, 42.] Later, the Lord comments: "He to whom
little is forgiven, loves little." [*id.* 47.]

* 62 *

THE mystery of man's confidence in approaching God freely is a matter of speculative curiosity, perhaps, when we consider Adam's *parrhesia* in Eden. But when we see the freedom with which the sinner approaches God in and through Christ, it is an entirely different matter: this is close to us, and it can be to us a matter of experience! Furthermore, this is the only *parrhesia* which we shall ever experience. The "free speech" with which God and man now familiarly converse together is and can only be the conversation that begins with, or implies, pardon. The *parrhesia* which can be ours is a greater gift than Adam's. It comes to us in the terrible yet healing mercy by which God gives us the courage to approach Him exactly as we are. One of the keys to real religious experience is the shattering realization that no matter how hateful we are to ourselves, we are not hateful to God. This realization helps us to understand the difference between our love and His. Our love is a need, His a gift. We need to see good in ourselves in order to love ourselves. He does not. He loves us not because we are good, but because He is. But as long as we worship a God who is only a projection of ourselves, we fear a tremendous and insatiable power who *needs to see goodness* in us and who, for all the infinite clarity of His vision, finds nothing but evil, and therefore insists upon revenge.

* 63 *

THE free and confident access of a soul that stands face to face with God and understands His mercy and is not consumed with self-hatred because of sins which, it knows, have already been consumed by His mercy—this is the *parrhesia* which is ours since the "goodness and kindness of God our Saviour appeared." [Titus 3 : 4.]

There are many examples of *parrhesia* in the Old Testament after the fall of Adam, but not the least significant among them is Job, who knew the holiness of God too well to avoid scandalizing his own holy friends. The frankness and volubility with which Job complained of his sufferings and refused to accept the pious rationalizations of his consolers were a paradoxical mark of his *parrhesia*, for the freedom of speech with which we approach God must be based on perfect sincerity and Job was perfectly sincere. His sincerity was recognized by the Holy One, Who answered Job out of the whirlwind, mocking the holy speeches of his religious friends. Chapters thirty-eight to forty-one of the Book of Job are a good example of man's *parrhesia* in which, incidentally, all the talking is done by God. The chapters are a hymn on the wonders of creation (through which God still continues His dialogue with man) and each new wonder named is put before Job in the form of a challenge and a question. This, indeed, is one of the characters of true *parrhesia*: it is a condition of freedom in which the inscrutable mystery of God speaks to us directly, challenging us with questions that do not have an answer. But in the end, Job himself, admitting that he has "above measure exceeded my knowledge" is not afraid, in his own turn, to ask the Lord a question. [Job 42: 4.]

This is because several times the Lord Himself has commanded him, "Gird up thy loins like a man: I will ask thee, and answer thou me!" *Parrhesia* is the fully mature condition of one who has been questioned by God and has thereby become, in the fullest and most spiritual sense, a man.

* 64 *

THE *parrhesia* which gave Adam free access to God in Paradise, and which also gives us access to Him in the new Paradise opened to the world by the Passion of Christ, was based on confidence in the truth of God's mercy. But the sin of Adam which robbed him and us of Paradise was due to a false confidence, a confidence which deliberately willed to make the option and experiment of believing in a lie. There was nothing in Adam's perfect peace that warranted this playing with unreality. There was no difficulty in the precept that had to be kept, to avoid falling into illusion. There was no weakness, no passion in his flesh, that drove him to an irrational fulfilment in spite of his better judgment. All these things would only be the consequence of his preferences for what "was not." Even the natural and healthy self-love by which Adam's nature rejoiced in its own full realization could gain nothing by adding unreality to the real. On the contrary, he could only become less himself by being other than what he already was.

All this can be summed up in the one word: pride. For pride is a stubborn insistence on being what we are not and never were intended to be. Pride is a deep, insatiable need for unreality, an exorbitant demand that others believe the lie we have made ourselves believe about ourselves. It infects at once man's person and the whole society he lives in. It has infected all men in the original pride of Adam. It has, as a secondary effect, what theologians call concupiscence: the convergence of all passion and all sense upon the self. Pride and selfishness then react upon one another in a vicious circle, each one greatly enlarging the other's capacity to destroy our life. In a sense, pride is simply a form of supreme and absolute subjectivity. It sees all things from the viewpoint of a limited, individual self that is constituted as the centre of the universe. Now everybody knows that, subjectively, we see and feel as if we were at the centre of things, since that is the way we are made. Pride however comes and elevates this subjective feeling into a metaphysical absolute. The self must be treated as if, not merely in feeling but in actual fact, the whole universe revolved around it. Concupiscence is then enlisted in the service of pride, to prove this one obsessive metaphysical thesis. If I am the centre of the universe, then everything belongs to me. I can claim, as my due, all the good things of the earth. I can rob and cheat and bully other people. I can help myself to anything I like, and no one can resist me. Yet at the same time all must respect and love me as a benefactor, a sage, a leader, a king. They must let me bully them and take away all that they have and on top of it all they must bow down, kiss my feet and treat me as a god.

Humility, therefore, is absolutely necessary if man is to avoid acting like a baby all his life. To grow up means, in fact, to become humble, to throw away the illusion that I am the centre of everything and that other people only exist to provide me with comfort and pleasure. Unfortunately, pride is so deeply embedded in human society that instead of educating one another for humility and maturity, we bring each other up in selfishness and pride. The attitudes that ought to make us "mature" too often only give us a kind of poise, a kind of veneer, that make our pride all the more suave and effective. For social life, in the end, is too often simply a convenient compromise by which your pride and mine are able to get along together without too much friction.

That is why it is a dangerous illusion to trust in society to make us "balanced," "realistic" and "humble." Very often the humility demanded of us by our society is simply an acquiescence in the pride of the collectivity and of those in power. Worse still, while we learn to be humble and virtuous as individuals, we allow ourselves to commit the worst crimes in the name of "society." We are gentle in our private life in order to be murderers as a collective group. For murder, committed by an individual, is a great crime. But when it becomes war or revolution, it is represented as the summit of heroism and virtue.

* 65 *

ONE would almost think that the great benefit modern man seeks in collective living is the avoidance of guilt by the simple expedient of having the state, the party, or the class command us to do the evil that lies hidden in our heart. Thus we are no longer responsible for it, we imagine. Better still, we can satisfy all our worst instincts in the service of collective barbarism, and in the end we will be praised for it. We will be heroes, chiefs of police, and maybe even dictators.

The psychological finesse with which the Fathers of the Church investigate the interrelation of pride, compulsive drives, anxiety and all the rest of the elements that evolve from the original act by which Adam wrecked the human spirit, is of great importance to ourselves.

Without going into too great detail, let us sketch out some of the broad outlines of the picture freely, following the thought of St. Bernard.*

*Sermons 81 and 82 in Cantica.

72

The act which was the source of all man's spiritual deordination was an act by which Adam cut himself off from God, from himself, and from the reality around him. It was the free rupture of the existential communion that not only made Adam fully real, but which gave him a part in all the reality that existed together with him. By an act of pure pride, untainted by the slightest sensuality, passion, weakness, fleshliness, or fear, Adam put an abyss between himself and God and other men. He became a little universe enclosed within himself, communicating feebly, hesitantly and fearfully with the other universes around him. The young worlds that came forth from him and Eve were wild, unpredictable and destructive worlds—beings like Cain that would have to be specially marked by God lest they be killed.

What was this sin? It was first of all an attitude of mind. No doubt there was some overt act which reached forth to eat the fruit of the "forbidden tree." But before the act was done, the attitude was there. It was a way of looking at reality that condemned man, by its very nature, to become unreal. What was the attitude? It was simply this: that Adam, who possessed an existential, an experimental knowledge of all that was good and all that was real, and who was mystically united with God, the infinite source of all actual and possible reality, wanted to improve on this by knowing something else, which, he thought, would be something more. In desiring to eat of the fruit of the tree of the knowledge of good and evil, he wanted, in fact, to add to the knowledge of good, which he already had, the knowledge of evil.* To be more precise he wanted to have an experience, an existential knowledge of evil. He wanted

*Cf. St Bernard, *De Duodecim Gradibus Superbiae*, c. 10.

not only to know evil by theoretical inference from good (which he could well have done without sin) but he wanted to know evil in a way in which it was not even known by God: that is to say, by *experience*. Now it was metaphysically impossible for him to increase his experience of the good by adding to it an experience of evil. In desiring what seemed to him to be more, he reached out for what was, in fact, disastrously less. In finding "two" he had less, not more, than the original "one." And he lost his inheritance, which was the free possession of all good, as a son of God. He tasted and saw that evil was terrible. And he hated himself for it.

It does not seem to me, however, that this act alone would have sufficed by itself to ruin Adam's spirit and destroy his union with God. That damage was done by all that was actually *implied* in the attitude leading to his sin. What was implied? I think something of a Promethean exploit was secretly implicit in the outlook that led Adam to eat of the one bad tree in the garden.* The fact that he was induced to "steal" the experience of evil by an act of disobedience clearly indicates, it seems to me, that he felt that all the good that had come to him could, if it were lost, be stolen back.

* 66 *

ADAM's pride was a kind of Promethean blindness to the true nature of love. He did not understand that the gifts which had been given to him could only be possessed as long as they were received as gifts. They were not and never

---

*It should be remarked that this was objectively a "bad tree" and not simply a good one which Adam was arbitrarily forbidden to touch in order that God's supremacy might be recognized.

could be won by right of conquest for that was impossible. To think otherwise was, in fact, completely to misunderstand the true nature of God.

Remember what we said above about Prometheus: thinking that the fire could be stolen, and not knowing it would be freely given, he unavoidably knew only false gods, not the living God. These false gods were beings only a little more strong than man, only a little more spiritual, only a little more wise. They needed fire, in the end, as much as man. They would resent the theft of fire. They would defend themselves jealously against any invasion of their Olympus. They did not want man to have what was theirs, for they could not afford to see themselves weakened and man strengthened. All these concepts imply a narrow, jealous, weak, fearful kind of god.

Now in stretching forth his hand to the bad fruit, that he might know evil by his own taste of it instead of merely by inference, Adam implied that the taste of evil was something God also might possibly be wanting. It was, perhaps, something God feared to let him have, lest man be made too strong and become His equal. (And yet Adam was already the equal of God in the fullest sense possible to mere man short of union with Him in the eternal beatific vision which was to be the reward of his probation.) Such a thought was only possible in one who had already ceased to know the true God.

Now St. Bernard puts this *sapor mortis*, this taste for death, at the very heart of original sin. It is the exact opposite of the wisdom, the *sapida scientia* or existential ("tasting") knowledge of the divine good. The two are incompatible with one another. They cannot exist together. Consequently, having acquired the one, Adam necessarily lost the other.

* 67 *

THE existential knowledge of the goodness of God is only possible when we experience the goodness of God in God Himself, that is to say, as He Himself "experiences" it. Our experience of His goodness is therefore an experience of infinite freedom, of infinite giving, infinite selflessness. It is invested however, in our own case, with one modality that differentiates this love as it is in us and as it is in Him. In Him, the love is *experienced as given* with infinite freedom. In us, it is *experienced as received* into the arms of our own finite and contingent freedom. But this modality, this sense of receiving, is tremendously important. For there is no full and total experience of God that is not at the same time an exercise of man's fundamental freedom (of spontaneity) and of God's mercy. It is a free consent in an act of mutual giving and receiving that takes place between two wills, two "persons,"* finite and Infinite. Finally, the only way in which we can possibly receive the fullness of divine love is to imitate His act of giving by surrendering ourselves completely to His love.

All these elements enter into the very nature of the *sapientia*, the supreme wisdom which is an experience of God, an existential communion in His own intimate life which is Love Itself.

* 68 *

ADAM, by his proud act, his insistence on "improving" his wisdom and science by adding to it the knowledge of evil, inevitably lost the full experience of goodness that was

---

*Actually, in the full Christian expansion of this experience, there is an awareness of the Three Divine Persons, distinct in their own personalities, each communicating to us that infinite Love which is the Divine Nature.

freely given to him by God. But he lost more than an experience. He lost his immortality, his contemplation, his power over himself and over irrational creation and finally even his status as a son of God. Along with all this he lost his immunity from disordered passion, his freedom from ignorance, his incapacity to suffer. These deprivations were not merely the revenge of an irate God—they were inherent in the very attitude and act which constituted Adam's sin. He lost his immortality: why? Because for him, life consisted precisely in his union with God the source of life. Breaking the contact between his soul and the source of life, and left to his own contingency, he himself became his own source of life. But he was a deficient source that soon ran dry.

He lost his freedom: not his freedom of choice, but his freedom from sin, his freedom to attain without obstacle to that love for which he had been created. He exchanged the spontaneity of a perfectly ordered nature elevated by the highest gifts of mystical grace, for the compulsions and anxieties and weaknesses of a will left to itself, a will which does what it does not want to do, hates what it ought to love and avoids what it ought to seek with its whole being.

Since he decided to depend on himself without contact with God, Adam had to become his own poor fallible little god. Everything now had to serve him, since he no longer served the Creator. But precisely, since he no longer fitted perfectly into the order in which they had all been established together, all creatures rebelled against Adam, and he found himself surrounded not with supports but with so many reasons for anxiety, insecurity, and fear. He was no longer able to control even his own body, which became to some extent the master of his soul. His mind, now, since it no longer served God, toiled in the service of the body, wearing itself out in schemes to clothe and feed and gratify the flesh and protect its frail existence against the constant menace of death.

The desire of earthly things, which are all destined for death, surrounded him with thicker and thicker shadows, and the soul that thus lived could see nothing around about itself but the pale face of death appearing like a spectre everywhere. . . . By enjoying perishable things as though they were its last end, the soul has put on mortality like a garment. The garment of immortality remains underneath, not cast off, but discoloured by the overcast garment of death.*

* 69 *

IF in the original fall we had simply been reduced to our own natural level, our condition would not have been so bad. We would indeed have been mortal, subject to ignorance and suffering and the rest: but we would have been able to resign ourselves to our fate and in some sense to adjust ourselves to it. For after all, human nature in its essence was not ruined, only weakened, by original sin. St. Bernard sees the fall not as a descent from the supernatural to the natural, but as a collapse into ambivalence in which the historical "nature" in which man was actually created for supernatural union with God is turned upside down and inside out, and yet *still retains its innate capacity and "need" for divine union.*†

The human soul is still the image of God, and no matter how far it travels away from Him into the regions of unreality, it never becomes so completely unreal that its

---

*St Bernard, *Sermon 82 in Cantica*, n. 3.

†That we have a natural need for union with God does not imply that our nature can demand that union as its fulfilment. But, as St. Augustine says, God has made us for Himself and our souls cannot rest until they rest in Him.

original destiny can cease to torment it with a need to return to itself in God, and become, once again, real.

* 70 *

THERE is a special anguish in the concrete concept of man that we find in the Bible, where man is never regarded as the embodiment of a pure, abstract human essence. When man is seen as an abstraction, his difficulties are easier to solve, his tragic dilemma can be spirited away, his anguish can be made to disappear. For if man is nothing but a rational animal, all he has to do is live reasonably and keep his animality under the control of his reason. He will thus be able to arrive at a certain natural tranquillity. He will be able to "find himself" at least in his natural dignity as a human being. He may perhaps even arrive at a knowledge of his remote Creator, knowing God as the cause of the effects that surround us on all sides. He may perhaps even "experience" God as the absolute justification for the ontological sense of being which sometimes springs up from the depths of our own soul. But, that, alas, is not enough. The inner recesses of our conscience, where the image of God is branded in the very depths of our being, ceaselessly remind us that we are born for a far higher freedom and for a far more spiritual fulfilment. Although there is no "natural" bridge between the natural and the supernatural, the concrete situation in which man finds himself, as a nature created for a supernatural end, makes anguish inevitable. He cannot rest unless he rests in God: not merely the God of nature, but the Living God, not the God that can be objectified in a few abstract notions, but the God Who is above all concept. Not the God of a mere notional or moral union, but the God Who becomes One Spirit with our own soul! This alone is the reality for which we are made. Here alone do we finally "find ourselves"—not in our natural selves but out of ourselves in God. For our destiny is to be infinitely greater than our own poor selves: "I said: You are gods, all of you sons of the Most High." [Psalm 81 : 6.]

The spiritual *anguish of man* has no cure but mysticism.

* 71 *

ADAM'S sin was a double movement of introversion and extraversion. He withdrew from God into himself and then, unable to remain centred in himself, he fell beneath himself into the multiplicity and confusion of exterior things; this is St. Augustine's view of the fall.* Adam turned human nature inside out and passed it on in this condition to all his children. Each one of us has the task of turning the thing right side out for himself, and the task is by no means easy. Whereas Adam started with his spirit centred in God and everything ordered to that supreme union, he first withdrew spiritually from God into his own soul, as if he could live in his spirit privately and alone, referring everything to himself instead of to God.

The practical consequence of this was that fallen Adam lived as if there were no common good in the world. His existential knowledge of evil involved him in a complete reorientation of his whole being upon a private good of his own which had to be first restricted to itself, entrenched within itself, and then defended against every rival. The fort in which he entrenched himself was his own body. No longer "spiritual," the body dominated his spirit. Henceforth his only contact with reality was through the openings in the wall of the fort—the five senses. But the senses only directly

De Trinitate, Bk. 12, ch. 8-10.

attain to material things. Hence Adam's spirit, submerged in the flesh, by that very fact became subject to and dependent upon matter. Now matter is in no sense evil of itself. Matter, like everything else made by God, including the body and its passions, is essentially good. But it is evil for spirit to be completely subjected to matter, for reason to be swayed and dominated by passion, and for the flesh to rule the whole man. Why? Because the flesh and the passions, of themselves, tend to anarchy, being at the mercy of sense stimulation, and hence responding blindly and automatically to every stimulus that presents itself. Spirit that is immersed in matter which it cannot fully control is therefore something like the captain of a ship that has lost its rudder and is carried away by the waves of a storm. The ship may well be a good ship, but it is lost.

The human soul in its fallen condition is worse however than the captain of a rudderless ship, because the captain can at least see that the ship is in danger. Our spirit, left to itself, is only dimly aware that it has been the victim of a disaster. It thinks, at first, that its condition is tolerably good. It feels to some extent at home in its own little universe —the body. It sets about its task of governing this universe with its own laws. Gradually it comes to find how little control it actually has: and how much it is actually governed by the blind needs and compulsive demands of passion. If it has doubted this for long centuries, psychoanalysis has made it no longer possible to doubt the tyranny that subconscious drives and compulsions exercise over the fallen human spirit.

* 72 *

RATIONALIZING and excusing the lusts and ambitions of a

selfish and fleshly ego, camouflaging its own defects and magnifying the sins of others, evading its countless fears, forcing itself to believe it own lies, the psyche of man struggles in a thousand ways to silence the secret voice of anxiety.

Having lost his realization of his true identity, man has exchanged the peace of innocent self-realization for the agony of guilt-ridden self-awareness. Instead of being perfectly actualized in spirit, integrated and unified in the selfless ecstasy of a contemplation that goes out entirely to the "other," man is literally "dis-tracted"—pulled apart—by an almost infinite number of awarenesses. He is conscious of everything trivial, remembers everything except what is most necessary, feels everything that he should not feel, yields to demands that he should never even hear, looks everywhere, pays attention to every creaking board and rattling shutter in his haunted house. For his soul and body, created to be a temple of God, cannot help but seem a haunted place after the desecration that has evicted its only rightful dweller. It is of no avail to try to exorcize the accusing silence by turning the place into a den of thieves. No amount of business prosperity and luxury can hide the abomination of desolation within us.

* 73 *

AFTER Adam had passed through the centre of himself and emerged on the other side to escape from God by putting himself between himself and God, he had mentally reconstructed the whole universe in his own image and likeness. That is the painful and useless labour which has been inherited by his descendants—the labour of science without wisdom; the mental toil that pieces together fragments that never manage to coalesce in one completely integrated whole: the labour of action without contemplation, that never ends in peace or satisfaction, since no task is finished without opening the way to ten more tasks that have to be done. How few of us have the honesty to cry out, with Ecclesiastes: "Therefore I loathed life, since for me the work that is done under the sun is evil: for all is vanity and a chase after wind. And I detested all the fruits of my labour under the sun...." [Ecclesiastes 2: 17, 18.]

Those are terrible words, we will not listen to them because they sound too much like despair, and despair is precisely the spectre we would like to keep buried in oblivion by our ceaseless activity. For in fallen man action is the desperate anodyne, assuaging the pain of a soul that instinctively knows that it was made for contemplation—a soul that knows that action, which is itself necessary, is only a means to that end.

* 74 *

IF we would return to God, and find ourselves in Him, we must reverse Adam's journey, we must go back by the way he came. The path lies through the centre of our own soul. Adam withdrew into himself from God and then passed through himself and went forth into creation. We must withdraw ourselves (in the right and Christian sense) from exterior things, and pass through the centre of our souls to find God. We must recover possession of our true selves by liberation from anxiety and fear and inordinate desire. And when we have gained possession of our souls, we must learn to "go out" of ourselves to God and to others by supernatural charity.

The first step in all this is to recognize our true condition.

Before we can ever hope to find ourselves in God, we must clearly recognize the fact that we are far from Him. Before we can realize who we really are, we must become conscious of the fact that the person we think we are, here and now, is at best an impostor and a stranger. We must constantly question his motives and penetrate his disguises. Otherwise our attempts at self-knowledge are bound to fail, for if we fully and complacently acquiesce in our own illusion of who we are, our "self-knowledge" will only strive to reinforce our identification of ourselves with this impostor.

Nevertheless, even the natural man is able, if he is honest, to make a beginning in the work of self-knowledge. Socrates used to go around Athens confounding the "right-thinking" citizens, the magistrates who assumed they knew who they were, the philosophers who imagined they knew the secret of words and of their power. In the end they killed him because he told them, too clearly, that they did not dare to face such questions. The judicial murder was committed in the name of the gods. But that was precisely the most eloquent admission of the fact that these people feared to face their own unreality, which they defended in the projected "reality" of gods in whom they could not really believe.

* 75 *

IT is a spiritual disaster for a man to rest content with his exterior identity, with his passport picture of himself. Is his life merely in his fingerprints? Does he really exist because his name has been inscribed in *Who's Who*? Is his picture in the Sunday paper any safe indication that he is not a zombie? If that is who he thinks he is, then he is already done for, because he is no longer alive, even though he may seem to exist. Actually he is only pushing the responsibility for his existence on to society. Instead of facing the question of who he is, he assumes he is a person because there appear to be other persons who recognize him when he walks down the street.

Since we are made in the image and likeness of God, there is no other way for us to find out who we are than by finding, in ourselves, the divine image. Now this image, which is present in every one of us by nature, can indeed be known by rational inference. But that is not enough to give us a real experience of our own identity. It is hardly better than inferring that we exist because other people act as if we existed.

* 76 *

JUST as some men have to struggle to recover a natural, spontaneous realization of their own capacity for life and movement and physical enjoyment, so all men have to struggle to regain the spontaneous and vital awareness of their *spirituality*, of the fact that they have a soul that is capable of coming to life and experiencing profound and hidden values which the flesh and its senses can never discover alone. And this spirituality in man is identified with the divine image in our soul.

St. Thomas gives us a concrete and thoroughly existential intuition of the divine image when he says that it is not only a static "representation" of something in the divine essence, but a *dynamic tendency* that carries us toward union with God. It is a kind of gravitational sensitivity to the things of God. "The image of God is seen in the soul in so far as the soul is carried, or is able to be carried, towards God."*

*Imago Dei attenditur in anima secundum quod fertur vel nata est ferri in Deum. Summa Theologica, I, Q. 93, a.8.

Now if we are to recognize this image in ourselves, it is not sufficient for us to enter into ourselves. It is not enough for us to realize that the spirituality of our nature makes us potentially god-like. The potentiality must be actualized. How? By knowledge and love: or, more precisely, by a knowledge of God that is inseparable from an experience of love. As St. Thomas says, in the context of the words quoted above: "The image of God is in the soul according to the knowledge it conceives of God and according to the love that flows from that knowledge."

Self-realization in this true religious sense is then less an awareness of ourselves than an awareness of the God to whom we are drawn in the depths of our own being. We become real, and experience our actuality, not when we pause to reflect upon our own self as an isolated individual entity, but rather when, transcending ourselves and passing beyond reflection, we centre our whole soul upon the God Who is our life. That is to say we fully "realize" ourselves when we cease to be conscious of ourselves in separateness and know nothing but the one God Who is above all knowledge.

We fully realize ourselves when all our awareness is of another—of Him Who is utterly "Other" than all beings because He is infinitely above them. The image of God is brought to life in us when it breaks free from the shroud and the tomb in which our self-consciousness had kept it prisoner, and loses itself in a total consciousness of Him Who is Holy. This is one of the main ways in which "he that would save his life will lose it." [Luke 9: 24.]

* 77 *

WHAT this means in practice is fidelity and attentiveness to the words of God. "He that is of God hears the words of God." To be "aware" of God is to enter into contact with One Who, infinitely hidden and transcendent, cannot be known as He is in Himself unless He reveals Himself to us. But God speaks to us, in His Scriptures, and has given Himself to us in His Son—our whole life of faith is a life of attentiveness, of "listening" in order to receive the word of God into our hearts. *Fides ex auditu.* And we listen to God in the Liturgy, in the Scriptures, in meditation, in every expression of His Will for us. "Not by bread alone doth man live but by every word that proceeds from the mouth of God." It is this listening and obedience to the word of God that restores the divine likeness in our souls, and brings us the truth that makes us free.

* 78 *

THE recovery of the divine image in our souls, in so far as it is experienced by us at all, is an experience of a totally new manner of being. We become "new men" in Christ, and we are able to verify the fact by the change in the object of our knowledge and in our manner of knowing. Indeed, when God is known in this sense, He is not known as an "object" since He is not contained in a concept. On the contrary, the mystical knowledge of God, actualized in the mirror of His image within us, mysteriously coincides with His knowledge of us: "I shall know," says St. Paul, "even as I have been known." [I Corinthians 13 : 12.] We apprehend Him by the love which identifies itself, within us, with His love for us. What will be fully realized in the beatific vision is realized inchoatively in contemplation even in this present life.

The recognition of our true self, in the divine image, is

then a recognition of the fact that we are known and loved by God. As such it is utterly different from any self-awareness, no matter how deeply spiritual it may seem. It is utterly different from any other kind of spiritual awakening, except perhaps the awakening of life that takes place within a man when he suddenly discovers that he is indeed loved by another human being. Yet this human awakening is only a faint analogue of the divine awakening that takes place when the "image" in our spirit comes to itself and realizes that it has been "seen" and "called" by God, and that its destiny is to be carried towards Him.

* 79 *

WITHOUT this inner awakening, which springs from the realization of God's merciful love for us, the image remains a mere potential likeness, buried and obscured, unappreciated because unseen. The image springs to life when, at the touch of God's ineffable mercy, it begins to take on its lost likeness to Him Who is Love. The presence of God in us is the presence of His likeness in our own spirit—a likeness which is more than a representation, it is the Word of God Himself, united to our soul by the action of His Spirit. The sense of being "carried" and "drawn" by love into the infinite space of a sublime and unthinkable freedom is the expression of our spiritual union with the Father, in the Son, and by the Holy Ghost, which constitutes us in our true identity as sons of God.

* 80 *

IT is quite usual, when a man comes into intimate spiritual contact with God, that he should feel himself entirely changed from within. Our spirit undergoes a conversion, a *metanoia*, which reorientates our whole being after raising it to a new level, and even seems to change our whole nature itself. And then, "self-realization" becomes an awareness that we are quite different from our normal empirical selves. At the same time we are vividly conscious of the fact that this new mode of being is truly more "normal" than our own ordinary existence. It is more "natural" for us to be "out of ourselves" and carried freely and entirely towards the "Other"—towards God in Himself or in other men—than it is for us to be centred and enclosed in ourselves. We find ourselves to be most truly human when we are raised to the level of the divine. We transcend ourselves, we see ourselves in a new light, by losing sight of ourselves and no longer seeing ourselves but God. Thus in a single act we accomplish the double movement of entering into ourselves and going out of ourselves which brings us back to the paradisiacal state for which we were originally created.

* 81 *

IT is a pity that this *metanoia* is so rare, often so completely unknown, in the lives of men. True, no natural power, no human ingenuity, no extreme of courage and generosity can suffice, by itself, to bring about this change of heart. It must be done by the work of God, the work of grace. It is a divine gift. But if the gift be rare, it is not because of any niggardliness on the part of an infinitely liberal God. It is because of our fear, our blindness, our ignorance, our hatred of risk. For after all, in order to make this leap out of ourselves we have to be willing to let go of everything that is our own—all our own plans, all our own hesitations, all our own judgments. That does not mean that we give up thinking and acting: but that we are ready for any change that God's action may make in our lives.

On this readiness to change depends our whole supernatural destiny. There are few true contemplatives in the world because there are few men who are completely lost to themselves and entirely available to love. That is to say there are few who are able to renounce their own methods of self-support in the spiritual journey towards God. This is as much to say that there is too little faith, even among religious men. Perhaps especially in them. For when a man comes close to God and begins to find out that the Lord is hidden in the clouds of an infinite and inexorable transcendency, he begins to be afraid of One Who is so completely Other.

* 82 *

GOD will not reduce the distance between ourselves and Him by any compromise with our own weakness and imperfection. With Him there is and there can be no compromise. The mercy, which is a total giving of His love to us, is anything but compromise, since it demands, in return, the total gift of ourselves to Him, and this gift of ourselves is obstructed, within ourselves, by our own self-alienation.

* 82a *

WHEN the light of God's truth begins to find its way through the mists of illusion and self-deception with which we have unconsciously surrounded ourselves, and when the image of God within us begins to return to itself, the false self which we inherited from Adam begins to experience the strange panic that Adam felt when, after his sin, he hid in the trees of the garden because he heard the voice of the Lord God in the afternoon.

If we are to recover our own identity, and return to God by the way Adam came in his fall, we must learn to stop saying: "I heard you in the garden, and I was afraid, because I was naked. And I hid." [Genesis 2: 10.] We must cast away the "aprons of leaves" and the "garments of skins" which the Fathers of the Church variously interpret as passions, and attachments to earthly things, and fixation in our own rigid determination to be someone other than our true selves.

THE SECOND ADAM

ALL that has been said so far about man being made in the image and likeness of God and therefore being made for union with God is incomplete and indeed remains meaningless for a Christian until we see it in its proper orientation— to the Person of the Incarnate Word, Jesus Christ. The whole theology of the Redemption, of man's supernatural vocation as a son of God, is summed up by St. Paul in his parallel between Adam and Christ: Adam the first man, the natural head of the human race and Christ the New Adam, the spiritual Head of regenerated and spiritualized humanity. But it is not enough, either, to reduce this parallel to such an obviously oversimplified statement: first Adam—second Adam. To say no more would be to imply, as preachers so often imply, that Adam was, so to speak, a "first attempt" that failed, and that the Lord was compelled to make good this first "failure" with a second attempt which succeeded, and which would not even have been necessary if the first had not failed. In this view, Christ would be in every sense "second" to Adam, except, of course, for the fact that He is God. He would be, in other words, an "afterthought."

This is by no means the view taken in the New Testament. Quite apart from the speculative argument that divides scholastic theologians on the question whether there would have been an Incarnation if Adam had not sinned, the New Testament writers clearly see Adam as completely subordinated and secondary to Christ, from the very beginning. Adam points to Christ. Adam without Christ is meaningless. The Fathers look at the whole economy of our Redemption from the point of view of eternity, and therefore they see it all as one integrated whole, centred upon Christ. Creation itself is orientated to Christ. Without Him, it makes no real sense in the actual order of things. Everything, past, present and future is contained in Him Who is the "Alpha and the Omega, the beginning and the end." [Apocalypse, 21: 6.] Adam's subordination to Christ is clear, because Adam is a scriptural "type" or prophetic "figure" of Christ, and it is a law of Biblical exegesis that the types in Scripture derive all their meaning and value from the anti-type to which they refer. Adam is therefore entirely subordinated to Christ, and without Christ Adam has no function and no meaning in Scripture. Without Jesus, Adam is merely the beginning of a story that wanders off inconclusively into nothing. Not only is Christ the term and fulfilment of creation, but He is also its source and its beginning. The far ends of time meet in His hands. He contains all extremes within Himself. He Who told the Jews, "Amen, Amen I say to you, before Abraham came to be, I am" [John 8: 58], might just as well have said: "before Adam came to be, I am." He is therefore not only the giver of a new life in the place of that which Adam ruined for us, but He is also the giver of the life which Adam received at the very first from the breath of God.

* 84 *

ALL men were united in Adam. All were "one image" of God in Adam. "Adam is in us all." We all sinned in Adam. Adam is saved and redeemed in us all. What does all this mean?

It means simply, as St. Bernard says,* that man's creation

*St. Bernard, *Sermon* 80 *in Cantica*, n.2.

in the image of God (*ad imaginem*) constituted all men as created "copies" of the Word Who is the eternal and uncreated Image of the Father. The potentiality in the human soul which makes man capable of being drawn to God is nothing else than a capacity to become more and more like the Word of God, and thus to participate in God's own vision of Himself. St. Gregory of Nyssa says: "The whole of human nature, from the first man to the last, is but one image of Him Who is."* When Adam was created in the image and likeness of God, we all were created in him, with a nature capable of being conformed to the Word of God. Therefore Adam, who contains all human nature in himself, and is therefore "humanity," is created in the image of the Image of God, Who has already decided, from all eternity, to become man in Jesus Christ. Hence in his very creation, Adam is a representation of Christ Who is to come. And we too, from the very moment we come into existence, are potential representations of Christ simply because we possess the human nature which was created in Him and was assumed by Him in the Incarnation, saved by Him on the Cross and glorified by Him in His Ascension.

* 85 *

WE are not used to the perspectives which enabled the Fathers and the New Testament writers to see the mysterious compenetration of all these realities in the one great reality of the Person of Christ. Consequently, without a certain schematization, we cannot grasp their meaning.

Let us begin by reminding ourselves of the great problem which has to be solved by our Redemption and divinization. Adam, created to live in God, to share the wisdom and

*Quoted in De Lubac, *Catholicism*, p. 5.

peace of God, lost the divine life for which he had been created in God's image. Once this union with God was lost, man had no way of regaining it by his own powers. Yet he could not be entirely happy left to his own nature since, in concrete fact, his nature, made in the image of God, cannot rest except in the perfect likeness of the Divine Word.

In order to return to God man had need of a Mediator —One who would unite in himself the nature of God and the nature of man, re-establishing in himself most perfectly the communion of God and man. Jesus Christ is this Mediator. Evidently His Mediation extends to more than our Redemption on the Cross. By His death on the Cross, Jesus bridged the gap that had been placed between God and man by sin. That was enough, no doubt, to re-establish human nature in the state of union with God which had once been the privilege of Adam. But if we look closer, we find that Adam himself has need of a Mediator. How else could he bridge that abyss, no less deep than the abyss of sin, which separates the created from the uncreated, the contingent from the Absolute, the nature of man from the nature of God?

In answering this question, the New Testament tells us that Christ is not only a Mediator in the sense that He obtained the pardon of our sins. Even before Adam existed, Christ was already a Cosmic Mediator. All things were created in Him and by Him and for Him. And He was, at the same time, already exercising another mediation which would include all men in Himself by His Incarnation. The very fact that men were made in the image of God meant that they were already potentially united with the Word of God Who was to come and take human nature to Himself. If this union were not already implicit, men could never profit by the redemptive mediation of Christ, which consists, precisely, in "dying with Him" and rising with Him from the dead. And this is only possible because we are all one with Christ, we are all in Christ by virtue of our humanity, just as we are in Adam by virtue of our humanity, by the very fact that we are made in the image of God, and possess that human nature which the Word of God took to Himself.

* 86 *

THE cosmic mediation of Christ is brought out clearly in St. Paul's Captivity Epistles, especially in the one to the Colossians. Here he says: "(Christ) is the image of the invisible God, the firstborn of every creature. For in Him were created all things in the heavens and on the earth. . . . All things have been created through and unto Him, and in Him all things hold together." [Colossians 1: 15-17.]

In reading words like these, one is astounded that they receive so little attention from Christians today. It is the Man-God, the Redeemer, Who is the "firstborn of every creature" and Who is consequently "born" before Adam. Christ comes before Adam not only because He is more perfect, has a more exalted dignity, a greater power, but also because in Him Adam is created, like everything else in heaven and on earth. All creatures, spiritual and material, are created in, through and by Christ, the Word of God. And He is "before all creatures"—their beginning, their source as well as their end. Furthermore, it is He Who sustains them in being. In Him they "hold together." Without Him they would fall apart.

* 87 *

THE whole character of the creation was determined by

the fact that God was to become man and dwell in the midst of His own creation. Creation is therefore not a pre-established fact into which the Word will come and fit Himself as best He can at the appointed time. Creation is created and sustained in Him and by Him. And when He enters into it, He will simply make clear the fact that He is already, and has always been, the centre and the life and the meaning of a universe that exists only by His will. To us, no doubt, this all seems very strange, because all the Gospel narratives of the Incarnation suggest that God enters into His own world as a stranger and an alien. But that is because we have our own peculiar ideas of proprietorship and possession. The hiddenness, the unobtrusiveness, the simplicity of Christ as Man are simply another manifestation of the simplicity, the unobtrusiveness and hiddenness of God Himself, living and acting in the world. God seems to us to be hidden not merely because of His infinite distance from us but also because of His nearness to us. He is closer to us than we are to ourselves and that is why we do not notice Him. It is harder for us to see Him than for us to see our own eyes. We can see our eyes at least in a mirror. Christ, the "light who enlightens every man coming into this world," is a light which we do not see, but which enables us to see. "In the beginning was the Word, and the Word was with God, and the Word was God. . . . All things were made through Him, and without Him was made nothing that was made. In Him was life, and the life was the light of men, and the light shines in darkness and the darkness grasped it not." [John 1 : 1-5.]

* 88 *

IF all things are created in Christ, and are therefore in

some sense contained in Him, much more is mankind contained and included in Him. If Adam, in whom we are all "one image of God," is created in Christ, then we are all one image of God, by creation, in Christ. Jesus, Who in becoming man does not cease to be God, is a Person in a different sense from other men. Unlike the mere human individual, Christ is not personalized by the individuation of human nature. His Divine Person can reach out and include all humanity in Himself without ceasing to be individual and distinct and without losing His own transcendent unity. All our personalities, all our individualities are derived from Him and sustained by Him both in what is most personal to each one and in what is common to them all. This not only by grace but also by nature. And this, once again, is all due to the fact that He is the uncreated Image of which we are created images.

* 89 *

Even if He had not become Incarnate, the Word would be the archetypal image of each human soul created in the image of God. But in His Incarnation, Christ assumed a soul which was, like our own, created and therefore *ad imaginem*. He Who is, as God, the perfect Image of the Father is, as man, the perfect likeness of His own divine Image. He is in fact identified with the image, consubstantial with the Father. Consequently he not only gives us a divine and ontological exemplar of our own spiritual being, but He presents to us also a created exemplar of spiritual perfection. And we shall see that the soul of Christ, united to the Word in a union closer than any other union of two natures that ever has existed or ever will exist, is not only the model of our existential communion with God, but is the *source of grace by which that union is effected in our own souls.*

Our union with God by grace is therefore, in effect, simply the reproduction in our own souls of the union between the created image in the soul of Christ, and the uncreated Image of the Word. How is that union effected in ourselves? Merely in a remote manner, by a kind of imitation? Merely by bringing our own minds and wills into conformity with a model outside ourselves? Not at all. Since we are created in the Word and are sustained at every moment by Him, the uncreated Image of God, in Whom we live and have our being, He is always present in the depths of our souls. This natural presence of the uncreated Image within us is enough to lay the foundation for a certain kind of natural contemplation which I do not intend to discuss here because it does nothing to "save" man—it cannot bring him to supernatural union with God. But our supernatural life in God is the ultimate perfection of the immediate union which already joins our own spiritual image of God with the uncreated and divine Image, the Word, within us. In other terms: the uncreated Image of God, which is God Himself, is present in the depths of our own souls as the source first of our natural life (which is independent of our own choice), and then of our supernatural life which depends on our own free response to God's love. Our natural union with the One God is an immediate existential union with Him residing in our soul as the source of our physical life. Our supernatural union with God is an immediate existential union with the Triune God as the source of the grace and virtues in our spirit. Our mystical union with God, finally, is the perfect coalescence of the uncreated Image of God with our created image not only in

a perfect identification of minds and wills in knowledge and
love but also above all knowledge and all love in perfect
communion. "I live, now not I, but Christ liveth in me!"

* 90 *

HERE we reach the highest point of the development of the
Augustinian doctrine of image and likeness. The one
responsible for this ultimate perfecting of Augustine's
teaching is the Flemish mystic John Ruysbroeck, and we
would do well to outline his theory here.

The mystical doctrine of Ruysbroeck is founded on the
theory of "unity of spirit"—first man's natural unity,
secondly his supernatural union with God by love and the
virtues and thirdly his perfect union with God "above all
graces and gifts."

First of all, let us look at the divine image in man as the
source of his natural unity within himself, with God and
with other men.

Our created life depends entirely and immediately upon
the uncreated life of God present within us, says Ruysbroeck.* Thus even our natural life is rooted in the divine
life of our Creator. It flows directly from the Image "Who
is the Wisdom of God, in Whom God knows His power,
His wisdom and His goodness." God lives in us by this
uncreated Image of His, and our life is the reflection, in our
own created image, of His presence in our soul. The natural
image in us imitates the Holy Trinity by its being, its understanding, and its tendency to return without ceasing, by
love, to the source of its being. This is simply the classical
doctrine of St. Augustine slightly modified.

*The quotations will be taken mostly from the French translation of his works
by the Benedictines of Wisques. Here we are following *Le Miroir du salut eternel*,
Ch. 17, vol. i, 123.

By this immersion of the created image in the uncreated Image, we live in God and God lives in us. We live by Him and for Him. Our natural life is hidden in God Who dwells in the substance of our soul.*

It is to be noticed that this uncreated Image of God is one and the same in all the souls that receive their life from Him. At the centre of our souls we meet together, spiritually, in the infinite source of all our different created lives. So, Ruysbroeck says:

We are all one life in God, in our everlasting image, above our created being. We are also one humanity which God has created and we are one human nature, in which God has imprinted His image in trinity, and which He in love took upon Himself so that He with us is God and man. And all men have received this alike, bad and good; for this is the excellence and exaltedness of our nature, and by means of it we are neither holy nor blessed.†

Clearly Ruysbroeck takes the words "man is created in the image of God" much more literally than we have so far taken them in this book. Instead of merely interpreting the words to mean, as did St. Bernard, that man was created after the pattern of the divine Word (*ad imaginem*) Ruysbroeck, while retaining the same thought, goes much further and says that man exists and is sustained *in* the divine Image Itself. That is to say: man's life is ontologically suspended from the life of God. Ruysbroeck is careful to make clear that his meaning is not pantheistic when he explains:

Thus we all have above our created being an eternal life in

*Ruysbroeck, *Le Miroir*, pp. 123, 134.
†From the *Twelve Beguines*, quoted by Eric Colledge in his preface to the *Spiritual Espousals* of Ruysbroeck (London, 1952), p. 17. Colledge errs in referring this passage to I Corinthians 15: 20-23 which deals not with man's natural life but his supernatural life in Christ.

God as in our living cause who has made and created us out of nothing. We have not emanated from God, according to nature, but God has known and willed us eternally in Himself; He made us not by a natural compulsion or necessity, but in the freedom of His willing.*

He is also careful to point out that this immanence of the divine life in us does nothing to diminish God's transcendence. "We possess this unity in ourselves and yet beyond ourselves."†

Now for our supernatural unity in God. From this same divine Image in whom we "live and move and have our being" (Acts 17: 28) there flows into our souls the grace that awakens knowledge and love, awareness of God, in our understanding and will. Now the divine Image not only dwells in us as our Creator, but He sends forth His Holy Spirit into our own spirit which becomes "one spirit" with Him. The *pneuma* we have met in the doctrine of St. Paul now appears as "unity of spirit" in Ruysbroeck. The Flemish mystic develops the concept to some extent, for he distinguishes between the *operative* unity of the mind and will with God, in acts of divine love and contemplation, and the *essentiated* unity of the spirit with God above all contemplation and understanding and love. But perhaps this corresponds to Paul's distinction between the mind (*nous*) and the spirit (*pneuma*) where both are informed and activated by the Spirit of God.

In supernatural union (union with God by grace) the divine Spirit within our spirit unites us immediately to the Image (the Word) in a new way. No longer is the divine Image present within us as unrecognized and known. We

*Le Miroir, p. 126.
† The Spiritual Espousals, Colledge, p. 89.

become aware of His presence. We plunge by supernatural understanding and love into the abyss of His light and being. And beyond all knowledge and love we are united with Him and rest in Him. Ruysbroeck says:

This higher life is the cause of all life and all sanctity. One may look upon it as a glorious abyss of the riches of God, as a living source in which we feel ourselves united to God, a source which springs up in all our faculties in graces and manifold gifts, each one receiving in particular what he himself needs according as he is worthy.*

One recognizes here the pure teaching of the Gospel expounded by a mystic who has entered into the fullest realization of the meaning of the New Testament not merely by studying its teaching, but by finding that teaching fulfilled in himself through the action of the Holy Spirit. Here we have, for instance the full meaning of the words of Christ in St. John: "He who drinks of the water that I will give him shall never thirst: but the water that I will give him shall become in him a fountain of water, springing up unto life everlasting" [John 4: 14] and St. Paul's: "Now there are varieties of gifts, but the same Spirit. . . . But all these things are the work of one and the same Spirit, who divides to everyone according as he will." [I Corinthians 12: 4, 11.]

This brings Ruysbroeck to our supernatural union with one another in God. Just as all men are naturally speaking one image of God and are united in the uncreated Image of God Who is the same in them all, so all the men who are sanctified by divine grace and have come to supernatural union with God in the Spirit and in Christ are one spiritual image of God. They form a much closer union by virtue

*Le Miroir, p. 125.

of the bond of charity which makes their souls one in Christ. This supernatural and spiritual organism of men who are one in the charity and faith of Jesus Christ is the Church, the Mystical Body of Christ.

The natural unity of men in the divine Image is therefore far different from their supernatural unity in Christ. First of all, the natural unity does, perhaps in rare cases become an object of consciousness, but ordinarily it is never thought of by men. Secondly, the natural union with the divine Image as source of our physical life does nothing, of itself, to sanctify us or to make us virtuous except in a very imperfect way which contributes nothing to our true happiness. Thirdly, although by nature we are united to God, we cannot be said to possess Him or to know Him as He really is and this natural union does nothing to reduce the distance of our exile from Him and from His Paradise. Finally, the fact that we are all united to God in one natural image and in one human nature has never contributed much to a true union among men. It cannot keep them from fighting and hating one another, from enslaving and exploiting one another and from destroying in one another the very image of Him they ought to love above all things.

* 91 *

CHRIST the Lord is called the "second Adam" and it is said that we live "in Him" by faith. What do these expressions mean? Let us glance at one of the principal texts of St. Paul on this point: "The first man, Adam, became a living soul; the last Adam became a life-giving spirit." [I Corinthians 15: 45.] And St. Paul explains the difference between them. Adam is of the earth. The life given to him by God, to be transmitted to us, is the earthly, physical life which gives us only a natural union with God as our Creator. It is true that Adam had the life of grace and of the spirit, but St. Paul prescinds from that in this text in which he is considering Adam's actual paternity—by which only natural life is transmitted to us. But Christ gives us more than a natural life. He is the source and principle of a life that is "heavenly," that is to say divine. The life given us by Christ is totally spiritual. He is a life-giving Spirit, not merely living in Himself with the fullness of both human and divine life, not merely enriched with all the fullness of grace and of the Spirit, but able also to communicate that fullness to us.

Just as Adam is the one chosen by God to preside over the first creation, Christ is sent by Him to institute and govern an entirely new spiritual creation. For with the death and Resurrection of Christ we are in a new world, a new age. The fullness of time has come. The history of the world has achieved an entirely new orientation. We are living in the Messianic Kingdom.

* 92 *

THE reorientation of all human life in a direction which is not immediately perceptible to the natural intelligence of man, is a characteristic work of Christ as the second Adam. It is the reparation of the harm done to the human race by Adam's fall. The second Adam comes down to find man in the depths of confusion, in the moral chaos and disintegration into which he has been plunged by the sins of the first Adam and of all our other ancestors. Christ finds Adam, the "human race," like the Lost Sheep and carries him back by the way he came in his wandering from the truth. The substance of the mission of Christ is to unite

men to Himself in the work by which God recommences
in the opposite direction the work undone by the first man.
Humanity, which was one image of God in Adam, or, if
you prefer, one single "mirror" of the divine nature, was
shattered into millions of fragments by that original sin
which alienated each man from God, from other men and
from himself. But the broken mirror becomes once again a
perfectly united image of God in the union of those who are
one in Christ. Thus, in Christ, "God reunites His whole
creation, including matter, but especially man, in a new
economy of salvation. He gathers up His entire work from
the very beginning to purify and sanctify it in His Incarnate
Son, the new Adam."*

Without this "recapitulation" of all mankind and indeed
of all creation in Christ, the creative work of God would
remain frustrated and vain. But in Christ the work done by
God in the beginning is renewed on a level of such lofty and
eminent supernatural perfection that we see, in the perspectives of the New Testament, that the first creation of the
world and of man was nothing but another of those prophetic
"types" or figures foreshadowing a reality far greater than
themselves: the reality of Christ and His Kingdom. The
creation of the world, of Adam and of Paradise is therefore
simply a shadow of that substantial reality which is to be
actualized in Christ, and His Mystical Body. In these
perspectives, the first creation is entirely secondary and
subordinated to the new spiritual creation effected in and by
Christ. This new creation begins with the Resurrection of
the Lord and will be perfected at the end of time. The
natural life and gifts imparted to man in the beginning were

*Mersch, *The Whole Christ*, Milwaukee, 1938, p. 230.

only the preparation for the supernatural life that was intended by God to be definitively his.

* 93 *

THE recapitulation of the work of creation sublimated and perfected in Christ is a communion in the divine life, an infusion of the life and glory and power and truth of God not only into man's spirit but also, ultimately, into all the material creation as well. The end is not yet attained, but it is in view in the spiritual vision of the Church who looks forward to the *Parousia* when Christ will not only appear on the clouds of heaven in judgment but will also at the same time shine forth through the transfigured trees and mountains and seas of a world divinized through its participation in the work of His Kingdom. This will be the definitive victory of life over death, and will be marked by that general resurrection in which matter will at last share in the triumph of life and of spirit and the bodies of the saints will bear witness, in their own glorified state, to the Resurrection of Christ. And so, in the words of St. Irenaeus:

The Word . . . by whom all things were made, in the fullness of time, to recapitulate and contain all things became man in order to destroy death, to manifest life, and to restore the union between God and man.*

The first Adam, by the irresponsible misuse of his freedom, by the act of original pride in which he substituted self-assertion for self-realization, had brought death, illusion, error, destruction into the life of man by awakening inordinate desire. The second Adam, by the perfect use of His freedom in obedience to the Truth, reintegrated man into the reality of the spiritual order. He

*St. Irenaeus, *Epideixis,* translation in Mersch, *op. cit.,* p. 232.

restored man to his original existential communion with God, the source of life, and thus opened again to him the closed gate of Paradise. Man was once again able to drink from the inexhaustible spring of truth which God had hidden in the depths of man's own nature at the point where the created image opens out into the uncreated Image of the eternal Reality—the Word of God. The work of the second Adam therefore restored peace to the soul of man by once again giving him secure possession of the life for which he was created. The victory of Christ over death has replaced the anxieties and the insatiable restlessness of fallen Adam with the tranquillity and completeness of the original *parrhesia* with God.

The "new life," the life of the Spirit, life "in Christ," is communicated to the spirit of man by the invisible mission of the Holy Spirit—a direct consequence of the Resurrection of Jesus. Therefore the "new creation" instituted by the second Adam is in fact a prolongation of His Resurrection. The new world which is called the Kingdom of God, the world in which God reigns in man by His divine Spirit, the world of the second Adam is, in fact, the aeon of the Resurrection—the new age that begins to dawn with the rising of Christ from the dead, which reaches out to touch, with the pure spiritual light of that dawning, each soul newly incorporated into the Risen Christ, until all the elect are gathered together in Him and the Kingdom is openly and definitively established without question and without opposition in the general resurrection of all the dead.

* 95 *

"IF," says St. Paul, "by reason of the one man's offence

death reigned through the one man, much more will they who receive the abundance of grace . . . reign in life through the one Jesus Christ." [Romans 5: 17.] That is exactly the Pauline concept of the Kingdom of God—a Kingdom of superabundant spiritual life, in which the saints "reign in life through the one Christ."

To reign in life is to have domination and autonomy by union with God as the source of life. It is to have and enjoy the sublime liberty of the sons of God, the freedom of the Spirit by which Christ has come to make us free. The early Church was entirely penetrated with this doctrine of liberation, plenitude and life. Wherever the authentic Christian spirit has prevailed, it has always been marked by this same perfect liberty and vitality in the Spirit. For always and everywhere the Spirit of Christ teaches this message to those who are His own: "For whoever are led by the Spirit of God, they are the sons of God. Now you have not received a spirit of bondage so as to be again in fear, but you have received a spirit of adoption as sons, by virtue of which we cry, Abba! Father! The Spirit himself gives testimony to our spirit that we are sons of God." [Romans 8: 14-17.]

In this view of Christ's role as second Adam, establishing the final victory of life over death, we are still confronted with the ideas of death and life together. The liberation from sin and death is effected by the death of Christ. The communication of life to our souls is effected by the Resurrection of Christ. "Jesus . . . was delivered up for our sins, and rose again for our justification." [Romans 4: 25.] We shall see that in order to enter fully into communion with the life brought to us by Christ we must in some sense—sacramentally, ascetically, mystically—die with Christ and rise with Him from the dead. The whole life of the Kingdom of God consists then in the gradual extension of the spiritual effects of the death and resurrection of Jesus to one soul after another until Christ lives perfectly in all whom He has called to Himself.

* 96 *

THIS great work of uniting the souls of the elect with their Head in one Mystical Body is the true task of the New Adam. The old Adam, without any effort on his part, came into being and found in himself all mankind, the whole of human nature. The New Adam, on the contrary, has to labour and suffer with great patience to unite to Himself, individually, each person who is destined to form a part of His Mystical Body. The New Adam creates himself, not only by the work and suffering and triumph of the Head, Jesus Christ, but also by the labours and sufferings and cooperation of each one of the members. The work by which Adam peacefully tended the garden of Paradise is replaced by another far more arduous labour, in another garden, in which (according to Pascal) Christ "is in agony until the end of the world"—although He is also triumphant and in glory. It is the work by which the New Adam painfully fights to establish his right to life by the conquest of death in each new member of His Body. Each one of us has his part in this labour, for we, in fact, are all the New Adam. We must never forget this active and dynamic view of the Kingdom of Christ. For if we are all "one man in Him" that does not imply that we float into heaven on the tide of His merits, without any efforts or merits of our own. On the contrary, if we did not join Him in His struggle to unite His members in one Body there would be no New

Adam at all. For if Christ were a Head without members, He would not strictly speaking be a "second Adam."

This will never become clear to us until we have realized the importance of the Resurrection as the completion and perfecting of the Passion. Christ's death on the Cross was infinitely more than sufficient to pay the debt of sin and to wipe out the offences of all men. It was also more than enough to purchase for us all the superabundant gifts of grace and glory necessary for us to achieve our destiny as sons of God. But unless we received these graces, unless we became united to His Person and through Him recovered our perfect likeness to God in "one image" and "one spirit," He would not effectively repair the damage done by Adam to the human race. He would not, in fact, be the second Adam, unless, rising from the dead and living in us as the principle of our supernatural life, He made us members of His own Mystical Body.

St. Paul makes this very clear in the context of the line we quoted above about Christ becoming a "life-giving spirit." The Apostle explains this line by urging us to live not only by the earthly and physical life we have inherited from Adam, but by the spiritual and heavenly life that is given to us in Christ. Thus, from images of Adam (the old man), we become images of the "new man"—Christ. "Therefore, even as we have borne the likeness of the earthly, let us bear also the likeness of the heavenly." [I Corinthians 15:49.]

* 97 *

How do we become like Christ? How do we bear His image? By living an "incorruptible life," which has its principle not in our flesh but in His Spirit—a life which is already an anticipated resurrection of our body. For "flesh and blood can obtain no part in the Kingdom of God, neither shall corruption have any part in incorruption." [I Corinthians 15: 50.] This means, of course, taking sides very definitely with the Spirit in that battle between flesh* and spirit which marks our mortal existence, "For he who sows in the flesh, from the flesh also he will reap corruption. But he who sows in the spirit, from the spirit he will reap life everlasting." [Galatians 6: 8.]

* 98 *

OUR whole person, body and soul, is raised sacramentally to participation in the Passion and Resurrection of Christ in Baptism, and this implies a preliminary interior justification by faith, which spiritualizes the soul in its intimate substance. The faculties of the soul nevertheless, as well as the body with its senses, remain subject to the "wisdom of the flesh." This demands an ascetic struggle, in which our spirit, united with the Spirit of God, resists the flesh, its desires and its illusions, in order to strengthen and elevate us more and more, and open our eyes to the full meaning of our life in Christ. Finally, however, there will come a mystical transformation in which we will be perfectly conformed to the likeness of Christ. The second Adam will live entirely in us. We will be "the New Man" who is, in fact, one Man—the One Christ, Head and Members.

---

*The word flesh is often used in St. Paul without moral implications, meaning simply the body as animated matter. In this sense the flesh is not evil. However, where there is question of the "flesh" sharing in the glory of the spirit, Paul generally uses the word "body" rather than flesh. In moral contexts, the word "flesh" means not only the animated body, but that body with all its inordinate passions, weaknesses and illusions and carnal desires, which militate against the soul, and are directly opposed to the influence of the "spirit"—Cf. Galatians 5: 16 ff.

* 99 *

THE recapitulation of all men in Christ implies the mystical union of all in Him, in one perfect image, one love, one freedom. "Now the Lord is the Spirit; and where the Spirit of the Lord is, there is freedom. But we all, with faces unveiled, reflecting as in a mirror the glory of the Lord, are being transformed into his very image from glory to glory, as through the Spirit of the Lord." [II Corinthians, 3 : 17, 18.]

This important text shows us better than any other how the effect of the Resurrection of Christ, His triumph and reign as the New Adam, is to manifest itself above all in the mystical union of all the transformed and deified members of regenerated humanity with one another and with God in Jesus Christ their Head. Here we see the sublime fulfilment of the mystery contained in God's original breathing of life into Adam. The spiritual life that was as yet not fully perfect in Adam, is to become one day, in us, a clear vision of God in the clarity of His uncreated Image seen without veil and without intermediary, face to face. But not only will this vision be a permanent discovery of Him Who Is—it will also be our own definitive discovery of ourselves in one another and in Him.

Here we see the real meaning of that self-realization in God which has been one of the main themes of the present book. We come to "realize" and "know" ourselves when we are fully actualized as we are meant to be in the designs of God. We are fully "alive" when we not only live perfectly in Him, but when we are aware of our life in Him—or, to put it more simply, fully aware of Him. Yet this awareness is arrived at through the plenitude of His Being reflected in the plenitude of His life in ourselves. We are most truly ourselves when our souls "reflect as in a mirror the glory of the Lord." And when a mirror is full of light, you do not see the glass—you are blinded by the light.

* 100 *

ST. PAUL says that union with God is common to "all the elect." "We *all* with faces unveiled. . . ." And, more important still for us in the present life, this union has already begun in us. He not only says that we will be transformed, but that we *are being transformed*. The degree and intensity of our transformation depends precisely on our union with the Holy Spirit, on the purity of the image within us. This, in turn, is a matter of charity. We are transformed by love, and transformed in proportion to the purity of our love for God and for other men.

* 101 *

THE New Adam is not only Christ, the Head of the Mystical Body, but also all those who, having the likeness of God restored in their souls, are His Mystical Body. These, as Pope Pius XII points out, in his Encyclical *Mystici Corporis*, form one Person in Christ. There is here "not merely a vague relation of dignity or authority" but of union which "forms one single and same organism":

The Mystical Head, which is Christ, and the Church which here below as another Christ shows forth His Person, *constitute one new man* in whom heaven and earth are joined together in perpetuating the work of the Cross: Christ, we mean, the Head and the Body, the Whole Christ.*

So it is that we ourselves are "the second Adam" because we ourselves are Christ. In us, the image of God, which is

Mystici Corporis, N.C.W.C. translation, §77.

complete and entire in each individual soul, is also, in all of us, "the image of God." The first Adam, "who is one man in all of us," is saved and transformed by the action of Christ and becomes, in us, the second Adam. Thus, with something of the compenetrative vision of the Fathers, we awaken to the deep and mysterious presence within ourselves of the first man and the last. We see that we ourselves are Adam, we ourselves are Christ, and that we are all dwelling in one another, by virtue of the unity of the divine image reformed by grace, in a way that is analogous to the circumincession of the Three Divine Persons in the Holy Trinity. God Himself dwells in us and we in Him. We are His new Paradise. And in the midst of that Paradise stands Christ Himself, the Tree of life. From the base of the tree the four rivers of Eden flow out to irrigate not only all the faculties of our soul and body, filling them with grace and mystical light, but also the whole world around us, by the invisible radiation of the Spirit present within us. We are in the world as Christ-bearers and temples of the Holy Spirit, because our souls are filled with His grace.

This, then, gives us a beginning of awareness of who we are. It is an awareness that is necessary for us to play our full part in the plan of God.

CHRISTIANITY is more than an ethical system, and it is clear also that the New Testament and the Fathers of the Church consider Christ to be far more than a "prophet" or a great Teacher. As the Son of God and the second Adam He is the Head and Life of the whole human race, and as such He is the principle from Whom flow into our souls all the strength and light which restore us to the divine likeness and make us sons of God, able to know and love God in the light of contemplation and to glorify Him by perfect charity towards other men. Jesus not only *teaches* us the Christian life, He *creates* it in our souls by the action of His Spirit. Our life in Him is not a matter of mere ethical good-will. It is not a mere moral perfection. It is an entirely new spiritual reality, an inner transformation.

Ontologically the source of this new life is outside and above ourselves, in God. But spiritually, both the supernatural life and God Himself Who gives it are in the centre of our own being. He Who is infinitely above us is also within us, and the highest summit of our spiritual and physical life is immersed in His own actuality. If we are only truly real "in Him" it is because He shares His reality with us and makes it our own. The reality which brings us into such intimate dependence on Him by nature is elevated by grace to a "unity of spirit," which, when it is fully perfected, amounts to a mystical identity.

Both these aspects of God—His transcendence which raises Him infinitely above us, and His immanence which establishes Him as the intimate centre of our own personal being—are experienced separately or even together in the existential communion to which our souls are awakened by the touch of the Holy Spirit. But until we begin to experience mystically the relation of the Spirit of God to our spirit as the Mover and the one moved, the action of grace tends to make itself felt in us as our own action. Nor does the ascent to mystical union drive a wedge between the soul and God: that would not lead to union but to division. In mystical experience the spirit of man is indeed aware of the reality of God as the "Other" immanently present within itself, but the more conscious it becomes of His reality and of His "otherness" the more also it becomes conscious of the union and "sameness" which unite Him to itself, and this is the great paradox without which mysticism would become schizophrenia, splitting man's whole personality and destroying him, instead of unifying and integrating and perfecting him in the highest degree.

* 103 *

WHEN we speak of "life in Christ," according to the phrase of St. Paul, "It is now no longer I that live, but Christ lives in me." [Galatians 2: 20], we are speaking not of self-alienation but of our discovery of our true selves in Christ. In this discovery we participate spiritually in the mystery of His Resurrection. And this sharing of the death and Resurrection of Christ is the very heart of the Christian faith and of Christian mysticism.

"I came," said Jesus, "that they may have life" [John 10: 10]. The life He came to bring us is His own life as Son of God. And because of His Resurrection He received the power to communicate to us all His Spirit as the principle of our own life and the life of our own spirit. The uncreated

Image, buried and concealed by sin in the depths of our souls, rises from death when, sending forth His Spirit into our spirit, He manifests His presence within us and becomes for us the source of a new life, a new identity and a new mode of action.

As we have seen, in speaking of the second Adam, this new life in us is an extension of Christ's own risen life. It forms an integral part of that new existence which He inaugurated when He rose from the tomb. Before He died on the Cross, the historical Christ was alone in His human and physical existence. As He Himself said, "unless the grain of wheat fall into the ground and die, it remains alone. But if it die, it brings forth much fruit." [John 12: 25.] Rising from the dead, Jesus lived no longer merely in Himself. He became the vine of which we are the branches. He extends His personality to include each one of us who is united to Him by faith. The new existence which is His by virtue of His Resurrection is no longer limited by the exigencies of matter. He can now pass through closed doors, appear in many places at once, or exercise His action upon the earth while remaining hidden in the depths of the Godhead: yet these are only secondary aspects of His risen life. The primary aspect of His risen life is His life in the souls of His elect. He is now not only the natural Christ, but the mystical Christ, and as such He includes all of us who believe in Him. As a theologian says: "The natural Christ redeems us, the mystical Christ sanctifies us. The natural Christ died for us, the mystical Christ lives in us. The natural Christ reconciles us to His Father, the mystical Christ unifies us in Him."*

*F. Prat, S.J.—*The Theology of St. Paul*, London and Dublin, 1957, vol. i, p. 300.

* 104 *

CHRIST living in me is at the same time Himself and myself.
From the moment that I am united to Him "in one spirit"
there is no longer any contradiction implied by the fact
that we are different persons. He remains, naturally and
physically, the Son of God Who was born of the blessed
Virgin in Nazareth, Who went about doing good, and
Who died on the Cross, two thousand years ago. I remain
the singular person that I am. But mystically and spiritually
Christ lives in me from the moment that I am united to
Him in His death and Resurrection, by the sacrament of
Baptism and by all the moments and incidents of a Christian
life. This union is not merely a moral union, or an agreement
of wills, nor merely a psychological union which flows
from that fact that I keep Him in my thoughts. Christ
mystically identifies His members with Himself by giving
them His Holy Spirit.

* 105 *

THE Divine Spirit purifies the image of God in my soul by
faith. He cures my spiritual blindness, opens my eyes to the
things of God. He takes possession of my will so that I no
longer remain the captive of my own passions and compulsions, but am able to act in the fruitful tranquillity of
spiritual freedom. In gradually teaching me charity He
perfects the likeness of God in my soul by conforming me to
Christ. For my union with Christ is much more than an
imitation of His virtues as they are described in the Gospel:
it must be a union created in me by the transforming action of
His own Spirit. And the Life which the Spirit breathes into
my spirit is Christ Himself, mystically present in my own
being and my own person. The supernatural life which

makes Him spiritually present in me is just as really my life as the physical life which makes Him naturally present in me. Both lives are gifts, both are intended for me by God since one is elevated and perfected by the other. Although the two can be considered as theoretically (*de jure*) separate, they are meant in the plan of God to be actualized (*de facto*) together, and both together are meant to bring me to my full stature and full reality in Christ. Both are necessary to make me the person God intends me to be.

But if my true spiritual identity is found in my identification with Christ, then to know myself fully, I must know Christ. And to know Christ I must know the Father, for Christ is the Image of the Father. The "identity" which begins to make itself known and felt within me, under the action of the Holy Spirit, is the identity of a son of the Father: a son who is re-created in the likeness of the only Son, Who is the perfect Image of the Father. The beginning of self-realization in the fullest Christian sense is therefore a sharing in the orientation which directs Christ, as Word, entirely to His Father. And here we truly enter into the deep mystery of God.

* 106 *

In the discourse at the Last Supper, Jesus was preparing His Apostles not so much for the Crucifixion, as for the risen life which they would share with Him when He would send them the Holy Spirit. These last chapters of the Gospel of St. John are at once so clear in their surface and so impenetrable in their depths that it would be ridiculous to speak of them as merely "sublime." There is no epithet that sums up their paradoxical combination of mystery and simplicity. The word "divine" ought to serve our purpose, but it has so often been abused that it has disquieting resonances. But whatever we say about these chapters the discourse at the Last Supper contains the very heart of Christian mysticism, that is to say of Christianity itself: for Christianity and Christian mysticism were, originally, one and the same thing.

* 107 *

When Jesus appeared to His Apostles after the Resurrection, He always came to them with the word "Peace" on His lips. This discourse at the Last Supper also begins with the "peace" of Christ: "Let not your heart be troubled." [John 14: 1.] The Christ Who said He came to bring "not peace but a sword," begins in these words a discourse which the Apostles find disturbing. He is on the point of starting on the strange journey which no one but He can travel. It is the journey from man to God—which is our own destiny. How shall we accomplish it? Only in Christ. "I go to prepare a place for you, I am coming again and will take you to myself; that where I am, there you also may be."*

Where is this place? It is not a place, it is God. In a sense, God is everywhere, in a sense He is nowhere. In a sense He is especially present in heaven, in another sense He is especially present in ourselves. Everywhere His presence is to us a mystery. Christ is about to enter upon the journey by which we are all invited to follow Him into mystery.

He says: "Where I go you know, and the way you know." The Apostles immediately protest. So do we. After two thousand years, we hardly know any better than they what

*I dispense myself from citing chapter and verse where the quotations come from the discourse at the Last Supper. They are all in St. John, chapters 14-17. References will only be given when texts are taken from other places.

Jesus meant. True, we have drawn forth something of the tremendous doctrinal content of these words: but are they any less a mystery for us than they were for the Apostles? If we think we see perfectly, after all our speculation, we deceive ourselves. We must always ask, with Thomas, "Lord, we do not know where thou art going, and how can we know the way?" Even though we already know the answer: "I am the way."

* 108 *

"I AM the way"—the words themselves are full of the silence of eternity and they impose this awful silence upon our concepts and upon discourse, warning us at once that analysis is not going to be enough. There is more in this than we can begin to analyse: for even a poor, familiar human personality in the end is beyond analysis. We can find out something about his character, but the *persona* that we see in him is the mask behind which the spiritual reality hides. And that reality can only be known by love. But here, we have more than a human person. We have a man who, mysteriously, is God. He does not expound to us a way. He Himself, eternal, divine, is "the way." And if He is the way, then, although He is the Truth and the Life, He is still not the end. He is the way to another. Who is this Other?

* 109 *

CHRIST, Whom we can see and remember and imagine, is the way to an unimaginable Father. The Beginning. The *Principium.* The End. From Whom the Word Himself IS, for Whom the Word IS. By Whom we are in the Word. For Whom we are. We have never seen Him. We have never thought of Him purely as He is in Himself. We cannot. He is hidden. He is unthinkable. We cannot name Him, until the Spirit of Christ, springing up within the depths of our own spirit, makes us know Him by making us sons: sons of the Hidden One, sons of the Beginning, sons of the Source, sons in the Word He speaks out of the infinite depths of His own unspeakable silence. Sons because, like His Son, our whole being knows it comes from Him and tends to Him Who is hidden, Who has "made darkness the cloak about him." [Psalm 17: 12.] This darkness is forever impenetrable unless the Father reveal Himself to us in the Son.* Even the Son is unknown to anyone but the Father. But the Son manifests Himself and His Father in the Holy Spirit Whom He gives to us. The Son, then, by the action of His grace in our souls, is the "Key of David" of which the liturgy sings in Advent. When His revelation opens our souls, no one can close them. When he closes them, no one can open them again. And He who alone has power to enter into the depths of our being, into those depths which lie far beyond our own domination, can there unlock an ontological abyss that opens out within us upon the darkness of the Beginning, the Source, the Father.

* IIO *

IT is thus that we "ascend" to the Father—by finding the Father within us as He is within the Son. "Thou Father in me and I in them. . . . In that day you will know that I am in my Father, and you in me and I in you." Clearly, whatever our knowledge of the Father may be, it is a sharing in the union of the Father and the Son.

*"All things have been delivered to me by my Father; and no one knows the Son except the Father; nor does anyone know the Father except the Son, and him to whom the Son chooses to reveal Him." [Matthew 11: 27.]

But what is that union? It is a union of two Persons in one nature. There is no division in the divine substance, no separation, no cleavage between the Father and Son. They are distinct, yet they are inseparably one. So much so that if we see the one (and we can see the Word Incarnate) we see the other, even if we do not pause to make the distinction of Persons. For they are one. After telling the Apostles that no one could come to the Father except through the Son, He added that they had already seen the Father, for they had seen the Son.

They, on the other hand, were aware of no such thing. They demanded to see the Father, in a cry that echoed the cry of Moses when he called out to the Lord, "Show me thy face. . . . Show me thy glory." [Exodus 33: 13, 81.]

And Jesus answered, Have I been so long a time with you, and you have not known me . . . ? He who sees me sees also the Father." He who sees Christ sees also the Invisible One. "Dost thou not believe that I am in the Father and the Father is in me?" And then Jesus goes on to say that the things He has done in their sight are the works of the Father and yet His own works. He immediately adds: "He who believes in me, the works that I do he shall also do, and greater than these shall he do." For Jesus must leave us, in His physical and natural presence, and go to the Father in order that by the Holy Spirit He may make both Himself and the Father present in us, and that the Father may live and act in us as He lives and acts in His own Son.

* III *

Our anthropomorphic imagination must not allow itself to complicate this teaching of Christ by imagining our union with God to be a kind of spiritual conclave of four persons acting together. When we are united with the Father, the Son, and the Holy Spirit, we are more "one" than when we are alone, for they draw us into their own unity of nature, and we share their unity with them in the reality of their own infinite act, which is One and unchanging and undivided and eternal.

* 112 *

IN saying that He is the "way" Jesus adds that He is the truth and the life. He is the truth, because the way is Truth, and in Himself He contains the Truth which is the beginning and the end. He is the life because, knowing Him, we live by Him as He lives by the Father. This communion in His truth and life immediately puts us on the "way" to the Father. We are in contact with the stream of life and power that flows from the hidden source, and ascending the stream we are making our way to the Source of life. The contact and the ascent are made through faith—faith which sees that Jesus is the Son and that He comes forth from the Father.* This faith sees that while Jesus comes forth from the Father, the Father remains in Him. And it sees that Jesus lives in us, and that the Father lives in us with Him. Christ is then the "way" to the Father because He brings the Truth and the Life of the Father into direct contact with our souls by sending His Spirit into our spirit, to make us one with Him.

* 113 *

AND now we come to the vitally important question of the free choice by which we ourselves establish this contact with Him.

*"I came forth from the Father and have come into the world. . . . They have believed that thou didst send me."

125

Let us recall something of what we have seen about the image of God in us. In God dwells the fullness of all reality and all perfection. He is therefore good, and blessed, by the very fact that He exists. But our contingent and created existence does not, of itself, imply goodness and happiness. We can exist, without, for all that, being what we ought to be. We can exist, in such a way that our existence is half drowned in the non-existence from which the creative act of God first drew us into being. We always tend by our contingency into nothingness and death. But at the same time we remain the image of the God of life. That is to say, we retain in our free wills the power to turn our whole being towards life rather than towards death. It depends on us to make ourselves real or unreal. Our vocation to become what we are meant to be implies therefore a trial of our will, a test in which we are questioned by God and make known our own free option. Our whole life is likely to be that test, and when we die we enter into His presence and give our answer—the answer that we have formulated by all the choices implied in the life that we have been living.

Freedom of choice is not, itself, the perfection of liberty. But it helps us take our first step toward freedom or slavery, spontaneity or compulsion. The free man is the one whose choices have given him the power to stand on his own feet and determine his own life according to the higher light and spirit that are in him. The slave, in the spiritual order, is the man whose choices have destroyed all spontaneity in him and have delivered him over, bound hand and foot, to his own compulsions, idiosyncrasies and illusions, so that he never does what he really wants to do, but only what he has to do. His spirit is not in command, and therefore he cannot run his own life. He is commanded by his own weak flesh and its passions—fear, greed, lust, insecurity, untruthfulness, envy, cruelty, servility, and all the rest.

He who is a slave is therefore never stable, never secure. He is always at the mercy of change. Therefore he cannot rest. He cannot defend himself against himself until he begins to make spiritual choices: and he cannot make any of these until he learns to resist the blinding compulsion of passion. In other words he cannot live like a man, by reason, until he trains himself not to live like an animal, by instinct. For since we are not meant to live by instinct, like the animals, our instinctive life is insufficient to sustain us at the proper level of our spiritual being, although it may be all right in itself.

If we are to live as free men in the supernatural order, we must make free supernatural choices. We do this by obeying God out of love. The discourse at the Last Supper is full of remarks about the importance of this obedience: but we will never understand the obedience preached by Christ unless we remember, always, that His obedience is not merely justice, it is love. It is not merely the homage of our wills to God's authority, it is the free union of our wills with God's love. We do not obey God because we have to but because we want to. That is precisely the nature of the free spiritual option that makes us sons of God. The Fathers of the Church, who contemplated the mystery of this freedom of the spirit, were perfectly aware that servility was incompatible with our divine sonship. We cannot become sons of God by an obedience that is merely a blind renunciation of our own autonomy. On the contrary, spiritual freedom consecrates our autonomy to Christ and, in Christ, to the Father, so that we may love the Father with His own spirit of freedom, or, so to speak, with His own autonomy. Where this truth is not grasped, Christianity dies and gives place to the legalism which nailed Christ to the Cross.

* 114 *

CHRISTIANITY is a religion of love. Christian morality is a morality of love. Love is impossible without obedience that unites the wills of the lover and the One loved. But love is destroyed by a union of wills that is forced rather than spontaneous. The man who obeys God because he is compelled to do so, does not really love Him. God does not want the worship of compulsion, but worship that is free, spontaneous, sincere, "in spirit and in truth." True, there must always be a limit where human weakness is protected against itself by a categorical command: "Thou shalt not!" There can be no love of God that ignores such commands. However, a true and mature love obeys not because it is commanded, but because it loves.

Christianity is not the religion of a *law* but the religion of a *person*. The Christian is not merely one who keeps the rules imposed on him by the Church. He is a disciple of Christ. True, he keeps the commandments of God as well as the laws of the Church, but his reason for doing so is not to be looked for in any power of legal decrees: it is found in Christ. Love is specified not by laws but by persons. Love has its laws, but they are concrete, existential laws based on values hidden in the very person of the Beloved. In the Sermon on the Mount, where Jesus compared the Old Law with the New, He introduced sanctions: but they were hyperbolical: "whoever says 'thou fool' shall be liable to the fire of Gehenna." [Matthew 5: 22.]* Jesus Himself,

*In Matthew 5: 21-26, sins are mentioned in an order of *decreasing* gravity, with punishments of *increasing* gravity. The implication is that we should not measure the sin by the punishment, but by the violation of charity involved in the sin itself.

living in us by His Spirit, is our Rule of Life. His love is our law, and it is absolute. Obedience to this law conforms us to Him as a Person. It therefore perfects the divine image in us. It makes us like God. It fills us with the life and liberty which He has taught us to seek. This is the value that determines all the actions of a Christian. This is the foundation at the same time of Christian humanism and of Christian mysticism: the Christian lives by love, and therefore by freedom.

* 115 *

IT is quite true that obedience to the command of Christ demands the sacrifice of our own will. But this is not to be understood as a sacrifice of true spiritual freedom. On the contrary, it is by renouncing our "own will" in the sense of a carnal and compulsive and deluded will, that we become spiritually free. It is in "obeying the truth" that we really find our true spiritual autonomy—

God has given to each one of us free will, the liberty of our own spirit, so that each might live not according to the unconditional domination of God but according to his own choice, not impelled by necessity, but guided by free will, so that there might be a place for virtue in our life and so that we might be different from the animals since, after the example of God, it might be permitted to us to do what we like. It is on this that is based the fact of a just judgment for sinners and a just reward for the saints and for the just*—

and in doing so we are united to God, by perfect love, in one will and one Spirit. St. Jerome brings out this aspect of Christian liberty quite clearly.

The gift of free will is therefore like a talent given to us by God and like the servants in the parable we are meant to

*St. Jerome, *Epistola* xxi, n.6.

use this talent, not bury it in the ground. We are meant to invest it in good actions, actions that correspond to our reality and our vocation, which make us at once more real and more free, so that by our liberty we come closer to God. But we remain free to destroy our own liberty by turning away from the source of life, from truth, from the way to God. A freedom that delivers itself to illusion is responsible for its own blindness and its own enslavement. But as long as it remains capable of choice, it bears witness to the fact that it is capable of finding perfect liberty in the love of God.

* 116 *

JESUS says that the man who lives by the divine life, who is born again of the Spirit and not of the flesh, lives by a mysterious and divine liberty: "The wind blows where it will, and thou hearest its sound but dost not know where it comes from or where it goes. So is everyone who is born of the Spirit." [John 3: 8.] St. Paul echoes the teaching of the Master: "Where the Spirit of the Lord is, there is freedom" [II Corinthians 3: 17], and Jesus also says, "The truth shall make you free." [John 8: 32.]

* 117 *

MUCH less speculative is the language of the Last Supper discourse and yet it is no less sublime. Here the liberty is the same transcendent liberty in the unseen Spirit. But it involves true obedience, and all that obedience implies of self-sacrifice. However, it is an obedience subordinated to love. It has no other sanction but love. "*If you love me*, keep my commandments." And immediately Jesus tells us, though in simple language, the same profound truth: that union of wills leads to a mystical union of persons. "He who has my commandments and keeps them, he it is who loves me. But he who loves me will be loved by my Father, and I will love him and manifest myself to him."

The writers who are fond of contrasting the Old Testament with the New—the Law of Fear with the Law of Love—have probably never thought that this statement of Jesus is simply a clearer repetition of the mysterious command originally given by God to Adam and Eve in Eden. "From every tree of the garden you may eat; but from the tree of the knowledge of good and evil you must not eat. . . ." [Genesis 2: 16-17.] Everything that has power to make us real, to bring us to the fulfilment of our destiny, to perfect happiness, and peace with ourselves and with one another, is contained in God's will for us: first His will as implanted in our very nature, and then His will as supernaturally revealed. To want to know something besides this one great good, to desire to add the knowledge of evil to the knowledge of good by turning away from God, is to turn away from life itself and from reality. We die the death.

* 118 *

CHRIST reopens the gate that was closed, barred and guarded behind Adam. By turning away from the experiential knowledge of moral evil, by seeking only that existential knowledge of good which is the exclusive right of those who know good by doing it, we re-enter the spiritual Paradise of God and prepare ourselves to realize His presence within us by contemplation. "Keep my commandments . . . and the Father will give you another Advocate to dwell with you forever, the Spirit of Truth whom the world cannot receive because it neither sees Him nor knows Him."

All the commandments of Christ can be summed up in

the one commandment—to love. We must love God and love one another. He who loves is free. He who loves is in possession of the truth. "The world" does not know this love.

The "world" is the body of those who hate, because they are prisoners of their own narrow illusions and petty desires. They cannot recognize the presence of the Holy Spirit because they are not willing to conform their lives to His inspirations. They cannot become free with the freedom Jesus compared to the unpredictable blowing of the wind, for they are rooted in their own attachments and bound down by their own compulsions. They have a fixed way of acting (which may be wild and erratic and possess a spurious "freedom" of its own) and they cannot break away from it. They have rendered themselves incapable of doing anything but their "own will" in the sense of their enslaved will. Only the Spirit Himself can penetrate their hard carapace of resistance, and too often they will not let Him do so. They are unable to love freely because they are afraid of freedom.

* 119 *

As long as men are "of the world" they cannot receive the Spirit, they cannot know Him. But Christ says to us "you shall know Him, because He will dwell with you and be in you."

There is only one sure sign of this indwelling: it is charity. "The charity of God is poured forth in our hearts by the Holy Spirit who is given to us" says St. Paul. And in his first epistle, John tells us: "No one has ever seen God. If we love one another, God abides in us and his love is perfected in us." [I John 4: 12.] "And in this we know that

132

he abides in us, by the Spirit whom he has given us." [*id.* 3 : 24.]

Commenting on these texts, the Fathers tell us that "if we desire the Holy Ghost with our whole heart, we have already received the Holy Ghost."* "Search the depths of your being. If they are full of charity, you have the Spirit of God. . . ."†

Those who love, know God. Those who hate show, by the very act, that they do not know Him.‡

This knowledge of God that is impossible without charity is not the mere knowledge of God the Author of nature. Even those who do not love can attain to a knowledge at least of His existence and of some of His attributes through His creation. But here Christ is speaking of that supernatural knowledge of God which implies a recognition of the Missions and Processions of the Divine Persons. To know God is *to know that the Word has been sent to us by the Father.*

* 120 *

To know the one God as the Creator of the universe is one thing. To know the Father as sending the Son and revealing Himself in the Son is quite another. The first knowledge is a knowledge "about" God, the second is a penetration into the infinite mystery of God Himself. We may truly apprehend something about God's love when we know Him as the source of our own being. But we learn, and learn by experience, that God is love—*Deus caritas est*—when we find that we ourselves have become identified with the Son Whom the Father has sent, and that the Father sends the

---

*St. Gregory the Great, *Homilia xxx in Evangelium.*
†St. Augustine, *In Epistola Joannis ad Parthos,* IV, §12.
‡John 16: 3, 15: 21.

133

Son from within ourselves, and that the Holy Spirit teaches us the identity of the Father and the Son. This Divine Spirit, leading us to oneness with the Word, enlightens us as to the infinite love which comes forth eternally from the Father as from a Beginning that has no beginning.

Now we begin to see the full meaning of Jesus' words: "I live, and you shall live." What is this life? It is eternal life, mystical life in the knowledge of "Thee, the one true God, and Jesus Christ Whom Thou hast sent." Much more it is the knowledge promised by Christ to the Apostles "in that day" when they should receive His Spirit. "In that day you will know that I am in my Father and you in me and I in you."

This last verse from St. John is a most complete expression of the unity of the New Adam. The Mystical Body of Christ is the Body of those who are united with one another and with the Father and the Son by a union of charity so close that it is analogous to the circumincession in which the Father dwells in the Son and the Son in the Father. Indeed, our status as sons of God depends on the fact that our unity with Christ makes the Father dwell in us as He dwells in the Son, while we dwell in the Father as does the Son. These theological expressions strive to express the most perfect possible unity. The man, therefore, who, enlightened by the Spirit of God, discovers in himself this union with the Father in the Son and with all men in Christ, is at the same time unified in the highest possible degree within himself and perfectly united with all who are one with Christ.

The force that holds this unity together is charity, and that is why everything that Christ tells us about union with God and the knowledge of the Father is centred upon charity. His own union with the Father depends on the love of the Father for Him. Our union with Him depends on His love for us, which is simply the extension of the Father's love, through Him, to ourselves. And the charity of Christ, which springs from the Father as from its hidden and infinite source, goes out through us to those who have not yet known Him, and unites them, through Christ in us, to the Father. By our love for other men, we enable them to discover Christ in themselves and to pass through Christ to the Source, the Beginning of all life, the Father, present and hidden in the depths of their own being. Finding Him, they who have long been torn and divided by the disintegrating force of their own illusions are able to discover and integrate themselves in one.

* 121 *

JESUS says: "As the Father has loved me, I also have loved you. Abide in my love. . . . Love one another as I have loved you. . . ."

It is possible to talk about charity without knowing what it really is: the word has been so distorted and so abused, so emptied of its original content. Christian love has been sentimentalized and debased, just as the idea of Christ Himself has been debased even by those who try to love Him.

We forget that He says "love one another as I have loved you," and not "love one another *as you have loved me.*" Our love, left to itself, is not always either very pure or very strong. To have strength, love must face realities. It must confront obstacles. It must accept difficulties. It must make sacrifices. It must be mature. Too often the love which we believe to be charity is merely an evasion of reality and responsibilities. It is the sentimental refuge to which we retire so as not to be bothered by the difficulties and hardships of life: a false sanctuary in which we are consoled by an imaginary Christ.

Jesus did not say He was creating an institution for the comfort and consolation of those who wanted to avoid the trouble of remaining fully alive. He promised us true life: "I live, and you shall live" but He also promised this life only to those who would follow Him through sacrifice and death to the resurrection in which life is beyond corruption. "For he who would save his life will lose it; but he who loses his life for my sake will save it." [Luke 9: 24.]

The patience and kindness, the meekness and humility, the self-sacrifice and devotion which are contained in Christian charity and are necessary for its exercise, are not and can never be the signs of a spirit of weakness and compromise that seeks only to avoid difficulty and to preserve peace at any price.

Nor is the patience of the charitable man merely a hidden weapon by which he shames and defeats his enemies. It is the strength which knows the difference between good and evil, and which knows how to overcome that difference by overcoming evil with good. Without this strength, this alchemy which silently and inexorably destroys evil, the passive aspects of Christian charity would have no reason for existence. They are never really negative. They are the negation of evil, and evil is a negation. Hence even the passive elements in charity are positive, constructive forces. Very often they are more constructive than the more obvious and affirmative acts of the charitable man.

* 122 *

THERE is all the difference in the world between the patience, the suffering, the sacrifice involved in charity and the patience, suffering and "sacrifice" displayed by weakness and masochism. The function of charity is to destroy evil, the function of masochism is to perpetuate it. Charity wipes evil out and replaces it by a positive, spiritual good. Masochism treasures and exploits evil as a good in itself, and loves suffering for its own sake. All that masochism requires that we do with suffering is dress ourselves up with it, decorate our souls with it, and use it as a pretext for taking a perverse pleasure in our own sterility. Charity abhors sterility, because it is the force which unites our souls with Life in its Source. Therefore it gives us a boundless capacity for productive thought, action and love. This is true not only in the exterior action of the apostolate or of works of mercy, but above all in the hidden and immanent activity which is contemplation.

* 123 *

CHARITY itself is the perfect argument for the fruitfulness of the Cross. For it is by the love that drove Him to die for us that Christ became able to live in our souls. It is by His death, inspired entirely by charity, that Christ destroys sin. And it is by loving other men, as Christ loved them, with a love as strong as death, that we too can destroy sin in them.

The Christian apostle should not make the mistake of thinking that the sinner understands nothing of this mystery of love, suffering, death and life. There is enough of the image of God in every man's soul to enable him intuitively to sense the presence of spiritual death under the exterior appearances of saintliness and of life.

If our preaching of the Cross is nothing but the expression of our own masochistic despair, those who hear us will not fail to be warned of it by their own instinct for life, if not by the Holy Spirit Himself. They will not be able to bear hearing us unless they are infected with the same disease themselves. Hence the terrible responsibility of every apostle to see that the charity that is in him remains alive and perfectly sincere. Who can flatter himself that he has succeeded?

We must at least know ourselves well enough to recognize our own illusions, our own limitations, our own weaknesses, enough to be able to tell when it is *not* the charity of Christ that speaks in our hearts, but only our own self-pity . . . or ambition, or cowardice, or thirst for domination.

That is why the New Testament makes sure that we always unite the thought of Christ's Passion with that of the Resurrection which is inseparable from it. The Apostles never speak of a death that is anything but the one narrow gate to a new life. Why? Because if Christ has simply died on the Cross, Christianity falls to pieces. The whole foundation of the faith is the Resurrection, not merely as a strong "apologetic argument," but above all in the sense that it is the objective basis on which the whole structure of the faith is constructed. "If Christ has not risen," says St. Paul, "vain then is our preaching, vain too is your faith. Yes, and we are found false witnesses as to God, in that we have borne witness against God, if the dead do not rise." [I Corinthians 15: 14, 15.]

* 124 *

THE reason for the crucial importance of the Easter mystery is, of course, the fact that by His Resurrection Christ lives in us. And by living in us, He manifests Himself in the love by which we love one another. For this love is the love by which He loves us and by which He Himself is loved by the Father. The whole purpose of His Mission among us is that the love of the Father for the Son be made known in our unity and that men may see that God is love.

This shows us how vitally important it is for Christians to understand something of the central mystery of their faith, and to build their lives not only upon a hope of avoiding sin, of carrying out the "practices of their religion," of dying on the right side of the law, but above all upon a knowledge of God and His love. If our Christianity is merely a set of exterior practices camouflaging a life of compromise with the weakness and hypocrisy of the world, we fail in our mission to manifest the hidden nature of God to men in our own lives. We fail to let people know, by the spirituality and purity and strength of our own lives, that God is love, and that He loves them all as He loves His own Son, and that He wants all men to recover their true identity as His sons.

"And the glory that thou hast given me, I have given to them that they may be one even as we are one: I in them and thou in me; that they may be perfected in unity, and that the world may know that thou hast sent me, and that thou hast loved them even as thou hast loved me."

SACRAMENTAL ILLUMINATION

* 125 *

"THAT which is born of the flesh," says St. John, "is flesh; and that which is born of the Spirit is spirit." [John 3: 6.] The phrase recalls that other text from St. Paul which we considered in an earlier meditation. Contrasting Adam who was of the earth, and Christ Who is the "man of heaven," Paul says: "Even as we have borne the likeness of the earthly, let us bear also the likeness of the heavenly." [I Corinthians 15: 49.] This means, as St. John explains, being born "not of blood, nor of the will of the flesh, nor of the will of man, but of God." [John 1: 13.] What is this new birth without which we cannot become sons of God?

We have already seen that the supernatural life is the reformation in us of the image and likeness of God by grace and divine love. But it remains now for us to consider precisely what agency brings about this change within us. It is faith, completed by Baptism. The "likeness" to God can only be re-established within us, in the image imprinted in our souls, when into that image we receive the light of Christ, the Word and Son of God. The process called "justification" (a juridical term that considers our elevation to the supernatural state from the point of view of the remission of sins) means little if it does not bring with it the healing and restoration of the divine likeness in us. It makes us spiritual men. And we have seen that the only way in which we can become "spiritual" in the true sense of the word is to possess within us a *pneuma* or spirit which is formed by the coalescence of our spirit with the Spirit of God in one principle of supernatural action.

140

WE become "spiritual" men (*pneumatikoi*) by believing in
Christ and by receiving Baptism. Thus we are "born again
of water and the Spirit." [John 3 : 5.] The act of faith, by
which we "die" to the evidence of mere unaided reason and
accept the inner light that comes to us from a source too
high for rational arguments to reach by themselves, immerses
us in the death of Christ in order that we may rise with Him
in the spiritual light of His Resurrection.

We are sanctified when we receive into ourselves His
"word," that is to say when we "take His word" about the
divine nature, about the fact that God is Love, that the
Father has loved His Son and sent Him to live in us, that
we may become in our turn sons of God, united with Him
as the source of our new life. "You are already clean," says
Christ, "because of the word that I have spoken to you."
[John 15: 3.] And this word is essentially the "word" and
the "name" of the Father. It is the revelation of the mysterious identity of Him from Whom all proceeds, even the
Son. "I have manifested thy name to the men whom thou
hast given me. . . . They have kept thy word. . . . The
words that thou hast given me I have given to them. And
they have received them and have known of a truth that I
came forth from thee." [John 17: 6-8.] "Sanctify them in the
truth. Thy word is truth." [John 17: 17.]

The sacraments (and Baptism is the first of them) are
protestations of faith.* They are signs of faith. They help
our human nature, in which the action of intelligence is
bound up with the work of the senses, to recognize and
express the inner action of spiritual forces which, if they are

---

Sunt autem sacramenta quaedam signa protestantia fidem, qua justificatur homo.
St. Thomas, *Summa Theologica*, III, Q. 61. a.4.

perceived at all, are usually only perceived in the most tenuous possible manner.

* 127 *

THE sacraments belong to the order of signs. They manifest something more than themselves, something hidden. Indeed, a sacrament is at once something visible and something hidden. The Latin word *sacramentum* is the normal translation of the Greek *mysterion*, or mystery. In each sacramental "mystery" we have an outward sign, an action, the application or use of some material element, or, in the case of the Eucharist, the Sacrament is permanently present in the consecrated Host, independently of whether or not the Host is consumed in communion. But also, in each sacrament, the outward sign is accompanied by an inward, spiritual reality, which it signifies. This inward reality is an effect produced by God in our soul, through the instrumentality of the sacramental action. And so the sacraments are very special signs, differing from other signs not only in their divine institution, but above all in the fact that they signify a spiritual reality, and at the very same time produce the reality which they signify.

At the same time, we must remember that the sacraments have a multiple signification. They point not only to a present spiritual effect in our own souls, but at the same time they link that effect with its cause, the mystery of Christ's Passion, and with its final end: the life of glory in heaven. Therefore in every sacrament we have not only a sign of the grace made present in the soul, but a sign of the Passion of Christ, which is the source and cause of that grace, and of the resurrection of all the saints in Christ, which is the term and fulfilment of all grace. Every sacrament therefore unites

142

in itself the past, the present and the future. It makes "present," in some way, the whole "mystery of Christ" by virtue of its own, proper sacramental signification.

* 128 *

THE richness of sacramental signification is not exhausted by the elements of the sacramental sign itself. Certain sacraments, like Baptism and the Holy Eucharist, are seen to be antitypes of mysterious events in the Old Testament which foreshadowed not only the coming of Christ but the sanctification of the elect in Him.

Just as Christ is the New Adam, so Baptism is a new Creation. Just as Christ is a new Moses, so Baptism is a new passage through the Red Sea. In the mystery of Baptism we are therefore brought face to face not only with the Passion and Resurrection of Christ but with all the great works of God from the Creation to the Last Judgment. We are mystically present at the deluge, at the passage of Israel through the Red Sea, at the entrance into the Promised Land, at the ascent of Elias in the fiery chariot (*merkabah*), at the Baptism of Christ in the Jordan, and at the mystical battles of the Apocalypse.*

* 129 *

IN the liturgy of the Oriental Church, the blessing of the baptismal font invokes the Creator, and recalls His presence, His power, in all created things by a beautiful prayer which reminds us that the same divine Wisdom Who made us is also to sanctify us and unite us with Himself.

*In order to appreciate a few of the typological figures of Baptism we have only to read the "prophecies" in the liturgy of Holy Saturday and the Vigil of Pentecost.

Before Thee the spiritual powers all tremble. The sun sings of Thee. The moon glorifies Thee. The stars meet Thee on their journeys, and the light listens to Thee. Before Thee the depths are aghast. The springs of water obey Thee. . . .

All creation sang to Thee when Thou didst appear among us. For Thou, our God, hast appeared on the earth and Thou hast lived among men. Thou hast sanctified the waters of the Jordan, sending down from on high Thy Holy Spirit.*

* 130 *

WE are "baptized in Christ's death" [Romans 6: 3]. As St. Thomas says,† the Passion of Christ is communicated to us in Baptism, as a remedy for our sins as if we ourselves had died on the Cross. At the same time, in Baptism, the power of the Resurrection flows out into our souls bringing us a new life in Christ. "But if we have died with Christ, we believe that we shall also live together with Christ. . . . Thus do you consider yourselves also as dead to sin, but alive to God in Christ Jesus." [Romans 6: 8, 11.]

Another important effect of Baptism is the sacramental character which it imprints on our souls. The baptismal character conforms us to the priesthood of Christ by an indelible spiritual sign which makes us able to unite ourselves with the worship by which the Incarnate Word, as Mediator between God and man, drew a fallen creation back into union with His Father. The sacramental character is, therefore, an orientation of our souls towards our Source and our Last End, in worship. But the character which unites us with the priestly action of Christ would do little to perfect our likeness to Him if our souls were not at the same time united to Him in a spiritual likeness and union by

*From *La Prière des Eglises de Rite Byzantin*, Chevetogne, 1937, vol. i, p. 344.
†*Summa Theologica*, III, Q. 69, a.2.

sanctifying grace. For it is by grace that we participate in His divine inheritance, become sharers of the divine nature [I Peter 1: 4] and sons of God.

* 131 *

THE grace and character of Baptism incorporate us in Christ, make us one with Him in His divine Sonship and in His priesthood. Therefore they make us members of His Church, His Mystical Body. Baptism is an initiation. Finally, and most important of all for our present subject, Baptism is an illumination (*photismos*).

"God is light," says St. John, "and in him is no darkness." [I John 1: 5.] The Word, the glory and splendour of the Father, is also the "light that enlightens every man who comes into the world." He is the light which is the "life of men." [John 1: 4.] This light shines in darkness, but unless God Himself draw us out of the darkness, we are not enlightened by Him, even though He be present. The illumination of grace by which we enter into the light is the effect of Baptism. To be precise, the light of grace in our souls is the light of Christ Himself, made present within us by His Spirit. In the words of one of the Greek Fathers, the soul is illuminated when the "Face of Christ" (that is to say His spiritual and transforming presence) fills the soul with its light and its lineaments as though He were reflected in a mirror.

Those who are illuminated take upon themselves the lineaments, the likeness and the true mind and appearance of the man Christ. The form of the Word is impressed upon them according to its true likeness and is begotten in them by sure knowledge and faith, so that in each one Christ is born. . . . They have become other Christs by their relation with the Holy Spirit.*

*St. Methodius in Rouet de Journel, *Enchiridium Patristicum*, 613.

THE depth of our soul contains, in its freedom and in-
tellectuality, the image of God. Freedom and understanding
are so to speak united in that summit of the soul which we
have called the spirit, as though in an inner sanctuary from
which they come forth to act in our everyday life. In the
spirit itself, our freedom and intelligence remain as latent
capacities for a supreme, spiritual activation which transcends
nature. The possibility of this activation is something of
which nature can only be faintly or remotely aware. It
cannot know what that activation is. But in aspiring for
perfect spiritual happiness, our freedom aspires to this
unknown perfection.

What happens when the soul is enlightened by God?
The summit of the soul is like a mountain top which has
been hidden in the clouds, but from which the clouds now
melt away, leaving the peak free in the clear upper air
through which it receives the full light of the sun. It is then
that the spirit of man, illuminated and transfused with the
presence of the Spirit of God and full of grace, becomes the
pneuma. Man's freedom and his understanding become
capable of a totally new dimension. They find themselves
able to aim their activity in a direction they had never
before known. New horizons open out to them—horizons
which are not below them, nor on their own level, but
above their own connatural powers. Yet at the same time
they have received virtues and gifts of God which, like
new instincts, prepare them to move in this new spiritual
field.

The spirit, the pneuma, is then strictly a "new nature."
The man who has become pneumatikos—spiritual—is
indeed a "new creature." And St. Paul was right to stress

the fact that this is the one essential thing in our religion. No rites, nor ceremonies, nor religious practices, nor codes of ethical behaviour are the essence of the spiritual life. This "new creature" is able to love God for His own sake because, by faith, it knows Him as He is. The "new creature" lives by the Spirit of Christ.

* 133 *

THE *pneuma* makes our freedom and our understanding sensitive to utterly new values, and capable of supernatural experience. Baptismal illumination may be understood by another image. It enkindles, so to speak, what the mystics of the High Middle Ages called the *scintilla animae*, or the spark of the soul. Thus sanctifying grace not only brings with it the bland, mild diffuse light which spreads over the whole purified atmosphere of the soul's summit, but at the precise peak of the spirit, the apex of man's inmost intellect and will, there now burns the white-hot point of mystical receptivity, that insatiable little diamond of spiritual awareness which is the most precious thing in the spirit of man—a treasure for which the world and all that is in it can only be thrown away and counted as loss.

What will happen to this point, the *scintilla*, when it makes itself felt within us? St. John of the Cross describes this "seed of fire" which is planted in the soul centred in God.

Who can speak fittingly of this grain of mustard seed which now seems to remain in the centre of the heart of the spirit, and which is the point of the wound (of love) and the delicacy of its delight? For the soul feels that there has remained within it, as it were, a grain of mustard seed, very minute, burning and full of power; powerful also and enkindled even to the circumference reached by its substance and the virtue of the point of the wound. . . . The soul is now conscious of the fitness of the comparison of the Kingdom of Heaven with the grain of mustard seed, made in the Gospel. . . . For the soul sees that it has become like a vast fire of love and the point of its virtue is in the heart of the spirit. *

* 134 *

THE sacrament of Baptism illuminates our soul with the light, and the presence, and the likeness of Christ. The divine image in us, our intellectual nature which is always obscurely in need of God because it is always hungering, even in spite of itself, for truth and for perfect happiness, now becomes the *pneuma*, the spirit. It knows where to seek truth, where to seek happiness. It has received the illumination that is necessary before it could begin its journey to seek Him. It has received the power without which it could not take a step towards Him. It has received the Spirit, Who is God Himself, and Who will teach it that the Father is close at hand, and He is to be found when we give ourselves to the inspirations of His grace. He is to be found in the action of our freedom, in the perfection of our intelligence—but not in the choices made by our natural free will, nor in the clear understanding of a naturally keen intelligence: only in the supernatural spontaneity of a soul that finds its supreme liberty in the liberty of the Holy Spirit and its total illumination in the darkness by which we travel into His light. Baptism opens the way to existential communion.

* 135 *

IN order to appreciate all these truths about the sacrament of

*St. John of the Cross, *Living Flame of Love*, II, 9-10, Peers translation, Vol. iii, pp. 44-45.

illumination, let us consider the liturgy of Baptism in the terms of the catechesis by which the Fathers of the Church explained, to the neophytes (the newly enlightened), the full meaning of their baptismal initiation.

There can be no more striking expression of Christian personalism than the rite of Baptism.

The first thing that happens is a dialogue between the priest and the catechumen, which takes place at the door of the church. The priest says "What is your name?" Then, when the catechumen answers, the priest addresses him directly by that name, and asks what he seeks of the Church of God. The catechumen answers "faith."

From the very beginning it is evident that the most fundamental question raised by Baptism is *man's true identity*. When an adult presents himself for Baptism (and the baptismal rite was originally framed for adults), he is supposed to have entered within himself, to have struggled as far as he could to dispel all his illusions about himself, to come to some rough answer to the questions: "Who do I think I am? What do I think I am doing? and Why do I think I am doing it?"

Christian illumination confronts a man, a spiritual creature of God, born to know God, a person who is yet not a person in the fullest spiritual sense of the word because he does not yet fully know himself. He is struggling to make his way out of the mists and confusion of error in which he is helpless to know himself. The confusion, the error, the illusion, the slavery of man's reason, pitiable, understandable though it may be, is still imputable in some measure to man's own will. No matter what may be the extenuating circumstances, every one of us has to admit that his blindness is largely his own fault.

AGAIN the priest addresses the catechumen by his name. There has been a short exhortation, during which the catechumen has presumably become lost in thought, and now he is recalled to himself, to the sharp, definite realization of his identity. One thinks, to some extent, of a doctor speaking to a man who is slowly coming out from a spell of unconsciousness repeating his name.

This time the question is: "Do you renounce Satan?" It is repeated three times. In the Oriental rite it is repeated more often, in different forms. "Do you renounce him?" Then, after a while, "Have you renounced him?"

Who is this other person who comes into the picture at this point? The Church has never compromised about her recognition of the fallen angels, man's spiritual enemies. What is important to her is not a given manner of imagining them or of trying to explain their nature. She is not obsessed with their identity, but concerned with the effects they produce in man's soul. Sin, the confusion that follows sin, the miseries, the self-hatred, the blindness, the almost infinite intricacies of delusion and error, everything that comes under the heading of neurosis and psychosis, all bear the mark of the devil: falsity, perversion, evil.

The one to be illuminated does not and cannot know his true self, cannot fully be himself, needs to be enlightened because he is imprisoned in the darkness of an error conjured up and kept in existence by the devil. Now this spirit of deception, by reason of the fall, is conceived by the liturgy as hiding in material things by which he is able to delude and ensnare the will of man. The Oriental liturgy of Baptism speaks of the Holy Spirit descending from heaven and sanctifying the waters of Jordan in which "the dragons had their nests." St. Cyril of Jerusalem in his *Catechesis* has a powerful symbolic description of the sanctification of created things by the Baptism of Christ. All creation was made holy by the fact that Christ descended into the waters of the Jordan and the Holy Spirit came down upon Him and upon the waters at the same time, driving out the devil. This sacramental action, in which evil was driven out of matter, and created things recovered their translucency in the eyes of man made innocent and spiritual once again, is symbolically presented as a battle between Christ and Leviathan. The picture was one that had deeply impressed the minds and imaginations of medieval artists.

The dragon was in the waters, according to Job, who says that he drank up the Jordan with his mouth. When, therefore, it was time to crush the head of the dragon, Christ descended into the waters and bound the strong one, in order that we might receive the power to tread upon serpents and scorpions. This was no small beast, but a terrible one, bringing death to all who met him. But life came to our rescue in order that death might be shut up in prison forever, and in order that we might all say: "O death where is thy victory?" By baptism the sting of death is taken away.*

This battle is fought again in the soul of the baptized man. Before the catechumen is washed in water and the Holy Spirit, the evil spirit is driven out of him—"the spirit of error, the spirit of wickedness, the spirit of idolatry and of insatiable greed, the spirit of lying and of all filthiness"† and then he is made ready to receive the Spirit of God.

First, however, the elect must declare his faith in Christ. For his recovery of his true identity, in supernatural life, can only be the effect of a free choice on his own part, an

---

*St. Cyril of Jerusalem, *Catechesis Illuminandorum*, 3: 11.
†Oriental rite, Fourth exorcism, *op. cit.*, p. 338.

act of his free will strengthened and elevated by the grace of
God. It is by this act, which is at the same time an option
and a self-dedication, that man enkindles within himself
that tiny spark which we have called the *scintilla animae*.
It will thereafter burn in the summit of his soul and guide
him to repeat these acts of free choice that lead him along
the desert road by which faith travels to God.

* 137 *

THE priest, once more addressing the catechumen by his
name, breathes on him, that he may receive the Holy
Spirit. Naming him yet again, he makes the sign of the
Cross on his forehead. Then follows a significant ceremony,
in which all the senses of the catechumen are signed with the
sign of the Cross. The words of the short prayers that
accompany this action indicate that by the power of the
Cross the spirit of man is to recover its lost spiritual senses,
and become able to penetrate, by mystical experience,
through the veil of darkness and mystery that separates us
from God.

"I sign thy ears, that thou mayest hear the precepts of
God.

"I sign thy eyes, that thou mayest see the brightness of
God.

"I sign thy nostrils, that thou mayest perceive the sweet
odour of Christ."

The Greek Fathers teach that the so-called spiritual senses
have very important functions in the interior life. They are
latent in our intellectual nature as seeds. At Baptism they
first begin to germinate. But they only develop when an
ascetic and sacramental life has purified us of the passions. It
is when the spirit is relatively free of dominance by exterior

sense impressions that it perceives, for instance, the spiritual sweetness of virtue by an analogue of the sense of smell and when, by spiritual "hearing," it understands the instruction given us by God through the *logoi* or natures of created things and by the action of His divine Providence in the world. These spiritual senses are above the level of imagination or emotion or any bodily sense whether exterior or interior. The whole point of the doctrine is the opposition between these senses, lodged in the intellect or in the spirit itself, and the senses of the body. The value of terms like "hearing" and "touch" is of course metaphorical. But the metaphor has some foundation in spiritual experience. There is, for instance, a real experiential justification for assigning the sense of the "presence of God" to the spiritual "touch," for it is like the awareness by which we "feel" the presence of a person near us whom we do not see. There is also a very good reason for saying that the quality of virtue is appreciated by the enlightened spirit after the fashion of a perfume or a good odour, and that we "taste" the goodness and mercy of God. Finally, it ought to be evident that the most perfect of the spiritual senses, which is spiritual "sight," should be proper to the spirit that is enlightened by Christ and experiences God and the Divine Persons as if it "saw" them, although it is still not blessed with that clear vision which is incompatible with life in the present world.

All these blessings are imparted to the several senses of man before Baptism itself, and the reason is that the spirit needs to be awakened and made sensitive to the great gift it is about to receive. Although most men may habitually receive the sacraments without much awareness of the spiritual impact of these divine instruments upon their souls, the Church always supposes that the sacramental life of the faithful should normally be heightened from time to time by deep perceptions of the reality of spiritual things. Nor is there any reason why this should not be so from the very beginning. The early Church, indeed, was familiar with the charismatic gifts imparted to the neophytes as soon as they received the Holy Spirit. And here we are not dealing with charisms but with "ordinary" grace.

* 138 *

WE must not underestimate the importance of this "opening" of the spiritual senses in Baptism. The opening of the ears (the sense of hearing being most intimately connected with faith) takes place again as the catechumen is about to enter the baptistery. But meanwhile his whole person has been blessed and signed and consecrated to the Holy Trinity, and a little salt has been placed on his tongue, that "the salt of wisdom may be unto thee a propitiation unto eternal life." "Wisdom" here of course implies an experience of the things of God, a deep knowledge of the ways of the Lord. It is perhaps not strictly the same as the contemplative gift described by St. Thomas. It has no doubt practical connotations which imply the prudent conduct of one's life, more than the repose of contemplation, but in the end one cannot escape the fact that the gift is conceived by the Church as in some sense mystical.

* 139 *

AT the baptistery, the calling of the catechumen by name is again repeated. He is again questioned three times, to make sure he has renounced Satan. All this does not imply that the Church has little confidence in her catechumens but simply brings home to us the fact that she emphasizes the element of *free choice* in our justification. And this brings us again to the main point: Baptism gives us our true identity, our spiritual existence in God. It makes us begin to be the person we are supposed to be, by uniting us with God through our own free option, by faith in Christ. It sets us on the road we are supposed to travel, if we are to fulfil our own individual destiny, and if our name is to mean anything. And all this is to be accomplished by the *affirmation of our own freedom*, elevated and transformed in the freedom of God. A "person" is one who leads his own life according to his state and his function and his place in the world. And so, in reminding the catechumen that he has a name, the Church reminds him that he also has a vocation. For to be named is to be called. And to be named by God is to be called, by a spiritual vocation, to a hidden identity that we will only fully realize when, in heaven, we receive the "new name" that no one understands but he who receives it.

It is after all these preliminaries that Baptism itself takes place, after a dialogue of lapidary but momentous simplicity.

"What are you called?"

The catechumen answers his name. And it is to be noticed that the phrase is not "what is your name?" but "what are you called?" What is your vocation? *To* what are you called. The answer is that I am called to be the person God wants me to be. I am called to be myself, and that is my vocation.

"N (repeating the name), do you believe in God . . .?"

"I believe."

He is questioned three times, for he must believe in the Father, Son and Holy Ghost. The identities of these Three Divine Persons enter mysteriously into his own identity when he becomes a Son of God. Finally the priest asks:

"N, *quid petis?*" ("What do you want?")

"Baptism."

"Do you want to be baptized?"

"I do." *Volo!*

The Latin is much more forceful than the vernacular. The idea is not merely that the catechumen "feels like" being baptized, or that he would like to be baptized but that he *wills* to be baptized. Here is a definitive, irrevocable affirmation of his freedom. An act of self-determination and of autonomy without which there would be no supernatural life. Without the free and conscious and clearly realized exercise of our own liberty we cannot become, in the full sense, persons.

* 140 *

IN the Oriental rite, even when Baptism is administered to infants, the neophyte immediately receives confirmation and the Blessed Eucharist. In the Latin rite, an anointing of the neophyte with chrism recalls the original practice of uniting Baptism and confirmation in one action. And so it is not out of place to speak of the descent of the Holy Spirit upon the soul of the newly baptized. In fact, without the invisible mission of the Holy Spirit into the soul there would be no Baptism. All that we have said of the spiritual senses would be without meaning. We are "born again of water and the Spirit." [John 3: 5.] St. Cyril of Jerusalem says: "When the water washes the body, the Holy Spirit sets His seal upon the soul, in order that with our hearts spiritually purified and our bodies washed we may approach God. Thou therefore who art about to descend into the waters, do not think merely of water, but by the action of the Holy Spirit receive thy salvation: for without both water and the Spirit thou canst not become perfect."*

St. Cyril insists that it is only this interior anointing with

Catechesis Illuminandorum, 3: 4. St. Cyril speaks of Baptism by immersion.

the Holy Spirit that can make us Christians. For when the Holy Spirit is "poured out" upon our souls we become "Christs" (that is to say "anointed ones") in all truth.

"Now you were made Christs by receiving the symbol (antitypos—sacrament) of the Holy Ghost and all things were symbolically wrought in you because you are figures of Christ. He also bathed Himself in the river Jordan, and having imparted the fragrance of His divinity to the waters, He came up from them, and the Holy Ghost in substance lighted upon Him, like resting upon like. In the same manner to you also, after you had come up from the pool of the sacred stream, was given the unction, the antitype of that wherewith Christ was anointed; and this is the Holy Ghost, of whom also the blessed Isaias says in the person of the Lord: 'The Spirit of the Lord is upon me, because He hath anointed me to preach His gospel to the poor.' "*

* 141 *

ST. CYRIL goes on to say that this descent of the Holy Ghost upon the soul completes our sacramental participation in the death and Resurrection of Jesus. And the Holy Spirit is truly present in our souls when our bodies are anointed with chrism. He explains how the presence and action of the Holy Ghost initiates us into the new world which can only be perceived by our spiritual senses. He shows how the Holy Spirit will live and act in us in the combat which must follow our Baptism, just as Christ was led by the Spirit into the desert to be tempted after His own Baptism.

And this reminds us of the fact that the sacramental illumination of Christian Baptism is not the end of a journey but only its beginning. The sacrament, the

*Catechesis Mystagogica, 3: 1.

"mystery", is not a mere ritual symbol that ceases to exist when the rite is terminated. It is the beginning of a new life, of which the ritual language of the sacrament has only given us the barest and most necessary outline. But that outline is enough to let us know that our souls have now been changed, and that we have received a new identity in God. The fire has descended upon us from heaven. We have not stolen it, like Prometheus. It has been given to us because the Father wanted us to have it, in order that we might find ourselves, and become His sons. More than that, the unction of the Spirit is given to our own free wills, in order that our liberty, in union with the liberty of the Spirit of God, may give glory to God in the creation of our own unique identity of which He alone possesses the secret.

* 142 *

"THE Kingdom of Heaven," says Jesus, "is like unto ten virgins who went forth to meet a bridegroom and his bride." [Matthew 25: 1.] The parable of the ten virgins tells us what the life of the Christian—and the life of the Church—must be in the present world. The sacramental illumination of Baptism has enkindled the lamp of our being, the *pneuma*. But out life is still a life of waiting in darkness. The vigilance with which we must expect the "coming of the Bridegroom" is the constant readiness to ratify the moral option made in our Baptism. The night of "this world" is the confusion, the routine, the mediocrity and the inertia of everyday existence with its distractions. When Christ tells us that the fundamental obligation of the Christian is vigilance and alertness, He is saying, in other words, that we must keep our liberty awake, ready at any moment to transcend the stultifying artificiality of common existence with decisions that affirm our inner, spiritual identity as sons of God.

* 143 *

THE virgins whose "lamps are trimmed" are those who, by faith, recollection, prayer, and self-discipline, keep the eye of their soul clear and simple: they remember that they have taken upon themselves full responsibility for their own moral life, and they are ready to account to God and to their own conscience for their use of their freedom.

The virgins in the parable are equally divided. Of the ten, five are wise, five are foolish. One sometimes wonders whether, in actual fact, the foolish are not far more numerous than the wise. It is all too easy to go through life with a supine and slumbering liberty that is like a lamp without oil—a lamp that does not give light when it is needed.

We most need the light enkindled in our spirit by the Spirit of God when the cry goes up "the Bridegroom cometh." And He comes not only at the end of time, at the *Parousia*, but also at unpredictable moments in our own individual lives—moments of crisis, when we are providentially summoned to surpass ourselves, and press onward to the fulfilment of our own personal destiny.

* 144 *

VIGILANCE in darkness is not only a frequent theme in Christian liturgical texts, but is an element in the very nature of the liturgy itself. The public prayer of the Church is precisely the lamp which she keeps trimmed, to bear witness to the light of her faith and to enable her to rise up and meet the Bridegroom when He comes. This is particularly true of the "Night Office" of Vigils and Lauds, which the monastic orders chant in the small hours of the morning.

Now the liturgy is meant to form the individual Christian. Hence we have to learn how to understand its symbols, in order to absorb the lessons which they convey. But at the same time the liturgy is more than symbolism and more than ritual. Through the medium of the Church, which He has entrusted with the task of guiding, sanctifying and instructing mankind, God exercises a sacramental action upon the spirits of men of faith. A theologian says:

With His divine fire [the Spirit] must gloriously change Christ's Bride into the image of His divine nature, transform her whole being by adding splendour to splendour, and pervade her with His own divine life. All this He must do so radically and so powerfully that it may be said of her that she does not herself live, but God lives in her. He must make her so like her divine Head . . . that she seems to be Christ Himself.*

The "lamp" of our own personal liberty is therefore fed with oil which is the doctrine of the Church and enkindled with the flame of the Holy Spirit Himself, through the grace which the Church bestows on us by means of the sacraments. The more we enter into the true spirit of the liturgy, the better we understand the "personalism" of our Christian faith. A mere outward conformism, a formalistic ritual participation in the ceremonies of collective worship not only does little to stimulate our interior liberty but even tends to stifle our freedom and stunt our spiritual growth. Why? Because it evades that interior option, that moral and spiritual self-commitment which the liturgy really demands of us. "This people honours me with their lips," says the Lord, "but their heart is far from me." [Isaias 29: 13.]

Freedom and slavery are incompatible. A spirit of servile conformity to rites and precepts, without the interior commitment of our whole selves to the consequences of a moral choice, obstructs the interior action of grace and prevents us from establishing a vital contact with the invisible Spirit of God. And by that very fact it prevents us from finding our true selves in the actualization of our own deepest capacity for charity and self-consecration. But in order to interiorize our spiritual activity we have to develop our awareness of spiritual realities. And this spiritual awareness, which depends first of all on faith, is also impossible if we do not have a genuine knowledge of ourselves.

*Matthias Scheeben, *The Mysteries of Christianity*, St. Louis, 1946, p. 544.

* 145 *

THE sincerity of all prayer, whether liturgical or private, depends on the fundamental acknowledgment of our actual spiritual state. We have to have some realization of what we are supposed to be, of what we are not, and of what we are. The first step towards a liberty that is a free gift of God's grace is the free acknowledgment of our own need for His grace. Or, in other words, if our liberty aspires to a union with the supreme freedom of the Spirit Who is Liberty itself, it must begin by freely accepting the truth about ourselves. For without truth we cannot see to make choices, and if freedom cannot see to choose, it is not fully free. We must see and accept the mystery of God's love in our own apparently inconsequential lives.

* 146 *

IT is not merely by thinking about the mysteries of faith that we can enter into them. We must dedicate our freedom to the course which they point out to us as the will of God. Without this dedication we will not only not understand them, but we will not even believe. It is only by acting upon the truths of faith, conforming our lives to their consequences, that we can come to make them our possession. And so, in the liturgy, in the sacramental life, we are taught as much by willing as by thinking. The intelligence and the will must always work together, more in faith than in any other virtue, but it is by the spontaneous option of our will that our intelligence lays hold on supernatural truth. In the language of the Greek Fathers, there is no true *gnosis* (knowledge of divine things) without *praxis* (moral and ascetic action).

* 147 *

WE only come to know God fully in and through Christ. And our knowledge of God through Christ depends on our spiritual union with Christ in the central mystery of our Redemption—His death and Resurrection. This is not only a truth which we accept as historical, not only a dogma which we believe: it is a redemptive fact which we must make the centre of our own spiritual life. This mystery, this redemptive fact, is the source and centre of all spiritual freedom. The option which raises our spirit above the half-alive level of mortal and material existence, and opens the way to a true and mystical life in God, is nothing but the effect of a direct contact between our soul and the Spirit of the risen Christ. The awakening of our spiritual liberty is impossible unless a movement of the loving and merciful will of Christ reaches out to touch and stir the depths of our own spirit. The deep option that makes us free, and thereby brings to life our true, our deepest self, is a resurrection of Christ in our own lives. It is the movement that our own will makes when it is mysteriously united with His, as if we were but one will, one person.

* 148 *

THE divinizing and transforming action of God is exercised upon our souls in a very special way in the liturgy. The Mass is the privileged centre of this divine action upon our inner freedom, because Christ is present, in the great redemptive fact of His death and Resurrection, whenever bread and wine are validly consecrated in the Eucharistic sacrifice. Those who participate in the sacrifice enter into the mystery with Him. "As often as this sacrifice is offered," says a prayer of the liturgy, "the work of our redemption is effected."*

The faithful die and rise with Christ in all their sacramental contacts with the risen Saviour, and in doing so they are made capable of experiencing the growth of spiritual knowledge and the increase of interior liberty which He has brought them in their meeting with Him. In this way they develop the gift of supernatural life that was imparted to them in Baptism. But this growth and development will never be complete unless they prolong these liturgical contacts by private prayer, meditation, asceticism and works of charity. The grace of the sacraments is given us to be not merely enjoyed but used. It is not merely to be thought about or looked at: it must be put to work. Only then do we begin to appreciate what we have received because only then does grace take hold upon our spirit, in the exercise of our interior freedom.

* 149 *

CHRISTIAN morality and asceticism are incomprehensible unless we remember that they have only one purpose: to enable us to grow in our existential communion with God, in the Risen Christ. I stress the word "Risen" because Christ, having crucified the Law in Himself, has risen precisely to bring us liberty—the liberty of His Spirit, the liberty of the sons of God, "the freedom wherewith Christ has made us free." [Galatians 4: 31.]

The morality of the New Testament all flows from this central fact of our liberation from the law by the death of Christ. The essence of this morality is its freedom. Its first

*Quoties hujus hostiae commemoratio celebratur, opus nostrae redemptionis exercetur. Secret, 9th Sunday after Pentecost.

obligation is that we preserve our liberty. How? By keeping
the great commandment which resumes and includes all the
others. "For the whole law is fulfilled in one word: thou
shalt love thy neighbour as thyself." [Galatians 5: 14.]

Clearly, love is impossible without freedom. Love that
is not free is not even love. Love's very life is spontaneity.
Therefore all the negative aspects of Christianity can be
summed up in the obligation to "stand fast and not be
caught again under the yoke of slavery." [Galatians 5: 1.]
Slavery, in this context, means servitude under a legal
system, bondage to the "elements of this world"—to
ceremonial and moral prescriptions which can do nothing,
of themselves, to bring men to interior and spiritual fulfilment. "If you are led by the Spirit, you are not under the
Law" [Galatians 5: 18.] But there is a far worse Law—the
"law of the flesh," with a worse slavery, beating down the
spirit of man "so that you do not what you would"
[Galatians 5: 17]. Both these servitudes, from which we must
keep ourselves free by the practice of a truly Christian life,
involve an immersion and absorption in what is below us.
The first imprisons us within ourselves in a fear that barricades itself behind legalism and superstition. The second,
while seeming to liberate us from ourselves, weakens and
stultifies our being in the confusion of fleshly licence. It
places a barrier between us and the very ones who share our
licence. True communion belongs to the spiritual order. It
cannot be consummated merely in the flesh.

* 150 *

WEAKNESS and fear are the elements that guide an enslaved
spirit, whether its servitude be that of frank licentiousness or
of apparent severity. "Perfect love," however, "casts out

fear." [I John 4: 18.] And unless fear be cast out, we cannot find ourselves because we will not even face ourselves. The truth that is in us remains the object of our greatest anxiety. We strive to keep it hidden from ourselves precisely because the truth will make us free, and we prefer to be slaves. Freedom brings with it too much responsibility—more than we can face by ourselves. But the Easter mystery tells us where we can find the strength to face it.

* 151 *

ONCE we enter again into contact with our own deepest self, with an ordinate self-love that is inseparable from the love of God and of His truth, we discover that all good develops from within us, growing up from the hidden depths of our being according to the concrete and existential norms laid down by the Spirit Who is given us from God. This mystical spontaneity (which begins with the free option of faith and grows with our growth in charity) sets the tone for our whole moral life. It is the inward promulgation of God's new law of charity in our hearts.

* 152 *

THE law of our life can be summed up in the axiom "be what you are." As sons and images of God, we must have no higher or more urgent obligation than to resemble Him in the purity, the universality and the perfection of our freedom in divine love.

The spontaneity of this inner "law" is like the organic law governing the growth of a flower or of a tree. When St. Paul talks about the "fruits of the Spirit,"* his metaphor

*"But the fruit of the Spirit is charity, joy, peace, patience, kindness, goodness, faith, modesty, continence. Against such there is no law." [Galatians 5: 22, 23.]

suggests something of the way in which a tree brings forth flowers and fruits without instruction, without command, without help from anyone.

Just as a plant grows and blooms and bears fruit by its very nature, in virtue of its intrinsic life-principle (or to put it differently, in virtue of itself, simply being what it is), so also the Christian virtues and works of love are viewed as the quasi-natural bloom and result of that new life which forms us into Christ and which the Christian receives at baptism.*

But although this spontaneity is "natural" to us in the sense that man was originally created with full freedom to live with God as though by a spiritual instinct, we have seen that our lost spiritual liberty is now no longer so spontaneous or so instinctive. It must be recovered by long and patient struggle.

* 153 *

WHATEVER may be the action of God upon our souls, whether He reach us through exterior agents or move us directly from within the depths of our own conscience, His grace means to bear fruit in our lives. This fruit is simply a more intense and better realized participation in the life of the divine Spirit. To put it simply, grace stirs up spiritual life within us. It awakens our faculties and impels them to fulfil themselves by transcending their present spiritual level. It calls us to reach out for a more abundant life, a fuller knowledge of God, a deeper sounding of the depths of our own selves and a more perfect and more generous giving of ourselves to the love and service of other men.

* 154 *

OUR life of "watching in the night," of sharing in the

*In Christ, by William Groussouw, Westminster, Md., 1952, p. 92.

Resurrection of Christ, which is the very essence of Christianity, the source of all Christian action and the centre of Christian contemplation, receives its most perfect liturgical expression in the Paschal Vigil. Here the Church renews her contemplation of the "Mystery" in all its fullness and in all its details. Here she calls to mind the whole truth of her mystical participation in the "*pascha Christi*"—the passage of Christ through this world to the Father. She renews the Christian "pasch," the passover, in which the freedom of man, led by God as by a pillar of fire, passes through the Red Sea of spiritual and material confusion to acquire its full autonomy. Here the Church is fully present to herself and present to Christ. She is fully conscious of her life in Christ. She reminds the faithful that Christ comes to them in the "night" of faith and tribulation of struggle and trial: and that they go out to meet Him by their own personal decision.

Holy Saturday begins the final phase of what one might call one great liturgy—a "Mass" lasting four days, renewing the whole sequence of the events of Christ's Passion and Resurrection. On Holy Thursday, the liturgy reminds us that every Mass is a representation not only of Calvary but also of the Last Supper. The mystery of the Eucharist is solemnly brought before us in its very institution. We see it as the Sacrament of charity—that charity by which we dedicate our freedom to God and to one another. At the same time, contemplating the betrayal of Christ by Judas, the Church recognizes that the seeds of betrayal are still in us all, for we all have in us something of the first Adam and of the sins which have caused the death of the Redeemer. On Good Friday there is no Eucharistic sacrifice and the Church does not die with Christ on the Cross, but rather

CALLED OUT OF DARKNESS

beholds His death in spirit, and laments the sins—our sins—
which caused Him to die. Holy Saturday is then a strange
new Sabbath, without Mass, a day in which practically
nothing happens, liturgically. The atmosphere of Holy
Saturday is one of numbness and inertia. It is a day of "rest"
not so much after the work done as before the work that is
to come. Here we are in the inexistential repose of dis-
orientation that precedes the great existential awakening of
Easter morning. Holy Saturday is a "rest" in a negative
sense—the rest of anaesthesia, of forgetfulness, of semi-
consciousness. It is a kind of sleep—the sleep of one who
has been down to the gates of death and is beginning to
recover. He has been far from himself. His sleep is not yet a
return to life, but it prepares that return. He will recover his
true identity again with the awakening of consciousness.
And that is precisely what happens on Holy Saturday night
when the liturgy "returns to itself" bringing back light out
of darkness, enkindling the lamps of the cold and empty
church, crowding back again to the stripped altars, and
jubilantly renewing the Eucharistic Sacrifice of the Christ
Who dies no more.

* 155 *

IN the cool darkness of the spring night the priest and his
ministers gather outside the door of the empty church.
The "new fire," struck from flint, is enkindled and blessed.
From this new fire the Paschal Candle will be lit. The
marvellous *Exsultet* will then be sung, proclaiming the full
meaning of the Easter mystery. Flame will be taken from
the great candle, and multiplied throughout the building
in all the different hanging lamps, and on the altar candles.
As Mass is being prepared, "prophecies" will be chanted

from various books of the Old Testament, showing how the types and figures hidden in the obscurity of the Old Law have been brought to light in the glory of the Resurrection. Each prophecy kindles a mystical light in the listening Church. This is a feast of light, a feast of life, celebrating not merely a past event but the present existential reality of the redemptive fact by which Christ communicates His life to us and unites us to Himself in one spirit.

* 156 *

ANIMATE and inanimate creation join with the Church in her feast. Not only men are present to solemnize the mystery, but angelic spirits join with them in the liturgical celebration. The texts that are chanted, the prayers and blessings, are the richest in the liturgical year. They are a compendium of theology—theology not merely studied, not merely meditated, but lived. Through the medium of the liturgy, the Word Himself, uncreated Truth, enters into our spirits and becomes our theology.

The first voice that speaks in the silent night is the cold flint. Out of the flint springs fire. The fire, making no sound, is the most eloquent preacher on this night that calls for no other sermon than liturgical action and mystery. That a spark should spring from cold rock, reminds me that the strength, the life of God, is always deeply buried in the substance of all things. It reminds me that He has power to raise up children of Abraham even from the stones.

The light that leaps out of darkness, the fire that comes from stone, symbolizes Christ's conquest of death. He, Who is the source of all life, could never remain in death, could not see corruption. Death is not a reality, but the absence of a reality. And in Him there is nothing unreal.

The fire that springs from the stone speaks, then, of His reality springing from the alienated coldness of our dead hearts, of our souls that have forgotten themselves, that have been exiled from themselves and from their God— and have lost their way in death. But there is nothing lost that God cannot find again. Nothing dead that cannot live again in the presence of His Spirit. No heart so dark, so hopeless, that it cannot be enlightened and brought back to itself, warmed back to the life of charity.

* 157 *

IN the old days, on Easter night, the Russian peasants used to carry the blessed fire home from church. The light would scatter and travel in all directions through the darkness, and the desolation of the night would be pierced and dispelled as lamps came on in the windows of the farmhouses one by one. Even so the glory of God sleeps everywhere, ready to blaze out unexpectedly in created things. Even so His peace and His order lie hidden in the world, even the world of today, ready to re-establish themselves in His way, in His own good time: but never without the instrumentality of free options made by free men.

* 158 *

THE blessing of the new fire tells us of all these things—of Christ, at once the stone and the fire from whom the spiritual light comes into the hearts of His believers. The fire that is blessed is not only a mystical symbol, but material fire "for our use." By the blessing of the Church the things that we use in ordinary life become sacramentals. They are already, by their very creation, symbols of spiritual realities.

The blessing of new fire is then a keynote of the whole

Easter Vigil—the new fire (says the prayer) is to enflame our hearts with heavenly desires, in order that we may be able with pure minds to enter into the feast of eternal light. The Mass is a figure of the festivity of heaven, at which our earthly liturgy makes us spiritually present.

In the blessing of the Paschal Candle, the Church calls upon God, the "invisible Father of new life," in order that His spiritual light may be mingled with the Sacrifice offered there in the night, and that it may go forth into every place where the consecrated fire may be carried.

* 159 *

THERE is nowhere in the Catholic liturgy a more wonderful praise of light and spiritual life than in the *Exsultet* which the deacon sings, with all solemnity, after the incensation of the Paschal candle. Heaven and earth are summoned to join in Christ's triumph. For the universe, beholding the sacramental fire, and perceiving beyond its symbol the spiritual and invisible light which is communicated to the whole earth through the Mystical Christ, feels the darkness of error and illusion slide away like a discarded garment. The Son, coming forth from the invisible Father, and dying on the Cross has washed away the debt of Adam in His own Blood, and in so doing has revealed the true significance of the paschal Lamb, and of the night in which the Children of Israel escaped from Egypt. He has united us to Himself in His victory. And then the *Exsultet*, surprisingly, becomes at the same time a hymn in praise not only of light but also of darkness. So profound is the meaning of the Resurrection that everything, even the purest negation, that is touched by its light, acquires something of a positive orientation.

Even darkness, even evil, even death, even sin: all of them, seen by the light of the sacramental fire, become capable of helping the work of God. They can contribute accidentally, but existentially, to the life, growth and liberty of our souls.

Christ died. But in the darkness of His death, He burst the chains of death forever. Those chains can no longer hold anyone who does not will, of his own free initiative, to remain their prisoner. Adam sinned, and because of the sin of Adam Christ died. Even sin, even the greatest of all evils, enters without discord in the new theological harmony of the *Exsultet*. The sin of Adam is no longer lamented. It is a "happy fault"—*felix culpa*, a "necessary" fault, that was "needed" in order that God's infinite love might receive its most striking proof and manifestation in Christ's death on the Cross. And the night, then: the night of inertia, anguish and ignorance, the night in which no man can see, no man can work? It has become a "truly blessed night" (*O vere beata nox*) which alone knew the time and the hour in which Christ rose out of hell. And here we come face to face with the existentialism of the Paschal Vigil—an existentialism which plunges through the very heart of the negative and the inexistential in order to find a reality too great to be contained in an objective concept.

This is the existentialism of the "apophatic" tradition: which contemplates spiritual realities not in light, not under clear objective forms, but in darkness, without form and without figure, apprehended only in the intimacy of the most personal and incommunicable experience. This night is brighter and clearer than any intellectual light that can appeal to our natural and unaided intelligence. It is the night of which it is written: "And the night shall become as bright as day"—the dark night of St. John of The Cross:

In the fortunate night
In secret, seen by none
And seeing nothing
Having no other light or guide
Than that which burned in my heart—

It guided me, this light,
More surely than the light of noon
To the place where he
Whom I knew well
Waited for me,
A place where there was
No one to be seen!*

* 160 *

BUT let there be no mistake. This "night" is not "beyond
good and evil" or beyond truth and error, in any sense which
implies an indifference to good and evil, truth and error.
On the contrary, the acceptance of "night" as the path to
light and union is simply the strongest affirmation of the
victory of good over evil, of truth over error, and of the
inexistential character of evil and of error. It is the passage
through non-being into being, the recovery of existence
from non-existence, the resurrection of life out of death. It
is the conquest which is demanded of every man who unites
himself with Christ: "Be not overcome by evil, but overcome evil with good." [Romans 12: 21.]

* 161 *

THE mystical night is not mere night, absence of light. It
is a night which is *sanctified by the presence of an invisible light*
(to which our visible, sacramental fire burning in the spring
night is only a witness). The brightness of the eternal light

*The Ascent of Mount Carmel, stanzas 3-4, translated from the Spanish.

is so great that we cannot see it, and all other lights become darkness by comparison with it. Yet to the spiritual man, all other lights contain the infinite light. He passes through them to reach it. And as he passes, he no longer hesitates, comparing one finite light with another, one empirical object with another, concept with concept. Travelling with haste, in the unerring security which transcends all objects, instructed by the Spirit Who alone can tell us the secret of our individual destiny, man begins to know God as he knows his own self. The night of faith has brought us into contact with the Object of all faith, not as an object but as a Person Who is the centre and life of our own being, at once His own transcendent Self and the immanent source of our own identity and life.

Other Books by Thomas Merton

No Man is an Island

This is a book about real things that are so solid we tend to ignore them. It proclaims the spiritual life as the life of our actual selves, as the truly real life. It asserts and insists the great truth that life must have a meaning. Thomas Merton shows that meaning as arising in the pursuit of our common destiny but as something we each have to work out for ourselves in our unique way, in fear and trembling.

This is a book about aspiration, asceticism and above all sacrifice— of oneself and of one's domination of self. It is about the choice between life and death, our last and most important decision: "Those who do not know there is another life after this one, or cannot bring themselves to live in time as if they were meant to spend their eternity in God, resist the fruitful silence of their own being by continual noise. Even when their tongues are still, their minds chatter without end . . . . How tragic it is that they who have nothing to express are continually expressing themselves like nervous gunners, firing burst after burst of ammunition into the dark, where there is no enemy." But ". . . the eloquence of death is the eloquence of human poverty coming face to face with the riches of divine mercy. The more we are aware that our poverty is supremely great, the greater will be the meaning of our death: and the greater its poverty."

"The author's most valuable achievement so far; it should find its place among the enduring works of Christian spirituality."—*Commonweal*

"A stimulating and strengthening experience. What he writes is the issue of genuinely personal thought and suggestive of a deeper than merely intellectual experience."—*The Month*

"By far the best thing he has done. It stands in a class by itself and deserves to hold a place among the great classics of the spiritual life . . . . This is a book by a mature monk who has been through the crucible and come out of it with wider horizons, a more balanced outlook and a more profound wisdom. It is the book of a monk who has learned much in the 'school of the love of God' and is concerned to pass on to others the fruit of his contemplation . . . . The author covers all the salient aspects of the spiritual life, and there is none that he does not illuminate."—*The Tablet*

published by Burns & Oates

Thoughts in Solitude

These inspired meditations form the sequel to *No Man is an Island*. Merton called them reflections on the spiritual life and the love of solitude. They are divided into thoughts on our solitude before God, our dialogue with God in silence, and the ways in which our personal solitudes are inter-related. Here Merton shows that spirituality is a supreme means of bringing the human personality to fullness and truth. Not only those whose calling is formally contemplative, but anyone seeking light and guidance of spirit in a world of discordance will find this book a lasting and profoundly effective guide to the development of his or her individuality. "In an age when totalitarianism has striven to devaluate and degrade the human person, we hope it is right to demand a hearing for any and every sane reaction in favour of man's inalienable solitude and his interior freedom . . . . Society depends for its existence on the inviolable personal solitude of its members. Society, to merit its name, must be made up not of numbers or mechanical units, but of persons. To be a person implies responsibility and freedom, and both of these imply a certain interior solitude, a sense of personal integrity, a sense of one's own reality." (*from the book*)

"Throughout the book, the sentences are pruned, weighted by their inner strength. Some of them are pure poetry. They have the ring of originality, the impact of *The Imitation*."— *The Sign*

"He possesses that rare talent for reducing the abstruse to the easily intelligible, without in the process watering it down."—*Jubilee*

"Compact and pointed...expressed in simple, graceful language . . . . The book is, indeed, a star performance on the part of Thomas Merton."—*Ave Maria*

Other Books by Thomas Merton

Bread in the Wilderness

This book of profound meditations offers not only serious religious interest but the contagious joy that is a constant characteristic of all Thomas Merton's works. *Bread in the Wilderness* is an account of what the Psalms mean to a contemplative who is also a poet; it is alive with joy.

Perhaps the most significant and influential collection of religious poems ever written, the Psalms sum up the theology of the Old Testament and serve as daily nourishment for those whose vocation is the life of prayer. Thomas Merton's classic study of the Psalms is like no other. This is no dull treatise but a glorious opening out of the riches of the Psalms for contemplation and personal prayer.

"The Psalms are more than language. They contain within themselves the silence of high mountains and the silence of heaven . . . . The Liturgy of Heaven is a most perfect harmony which, like the music of the spheres, sees song transfigured into silence. The Psalter is the prelude to that Liturgy." (*from the book*)

The Living Bread

This book is a series of moving and resonant meditations on Christianity as Christ himself living in unity with persons of good will. *The Living Bread* is a lasting exposition of the central truth of the Eucharist as the sacrament of love. This is no dull doctrinal compendium but a powerful document of the spirit asserting the unmistakable relevance of eternal truth to the present moment: "The whole problem of our time is the problem of love. How are we going to recover the ability to love ourselves and to love one another?...We cannot be at peace with others because we are not at peace with ourselves, and we cannot be at peace with ourselves because we are not at peace with God . . . . To find God one must first be free . . . . To conquer the forces of death and despair, we must unite ourselves mystically to Christ who has overcome death and who brings us life and hope . . . . This book is not a defence of a doctrine, but a meditation on a sacred mystery."

published by Burns & Oates

The Ascent to Truth

This book is a journey towards the highest summit of knowledge—
ultimate truth. In showing that this summit of truth is reached in
contemplation, Thomas Merton offers a brilliant exposition of the
doctrines of St John of the Cross, the sixteenth-century Carmelite
mystic, poet and theologian who became a Doctor of the Church.
Mystical contemplation is symbolized as the "dark night of the soul"
which Moses experienced on Mount Sinai in his three visions of God
as fire, cloud and darkness. "The paradox of contemplation..."
Merton says, "is that God is never fully known unless He is loved. . . .
Because he is without love, modern man is incapable of seeing the only
Truth that matters."

"The work of a man of clear intellect, who has made a choice and can
explain why he has made it."—*The Observer*

"Inspirational writing on a very high plane."—*The New Yorker*

Raids on the Unspeakable

This powerful book reveals a Merton directly and deeply engaged with
the critical situation of men and women in our present-day world. In
these brief but challenging pieces Merton does not offer cheap
consolation or easy remedies. He looks candidly and without illusions
at the world we have made. Though he sees dark horizons, his ultimate
answer is one of Christian hope. To vary the perspective, he writes in
many forms, using parable and myth, the essay and the meditation,
satire and manifesto, prose poetry and adaptations from a medieval
Arab mystic, to humanize and dramatize his themes. And there are
essays inspired by the work of contemporary writers. This is the
mature Merton writing at the height of his powers, with full intensity
of heart and out of deep compassion for a world sadly awry yet always
offering signs of hope.

Other Books by Thomas Merton

Conjectures of a Guilty Bystander

"Maybe the best way to characterize this book is to say that it consists of a series of sketches and meditations, some poetic and literary, others historical and even theological, fitted together in a spontaneous, informal philosophic scheme in such a way that they react upon each other. The total result is a personal and monastic meditation, a testimony of Christian reflection... a confrontation of twentieth-century questions in the light of a monastic commitment, which inevitably makes one something of a 'bystander.'"

Based on the journals Merton kept from 1956 to late 1965, three years before his tragic death in 1968, this series of comments on questions of that time and others very much reflects the author's view of the Second Vatican Council and its implications for the Church: "If the Catholic Church is turning to the modern world and to the other Christian churches, and if she is perhaps for the first time seriously taking note of the non-Christian religions on their own terms, then it becomes necessary for at least a few contemplative and monastic theologians to contribute something of their own to the discussion. That is one of the things this book attempts to do. It gives a monastic and personal view of these contemporary questions. The singular, existential, poetic approach is proper to this monastic view."

Such reflections are interspersed with views on writers as diverse as Camus, Gandhi, Bonhoeffer, Teilhard de Chardin, and many others. Light relief is provided by sparkling and humorous anecdotes of life in the monastery.

This is the mature Merton at his best—detached but not dispassionate, humorous yet sensitive, searching and alive—and all expressed with the facility of language that has made him still one of the most widely read spiritual writers of the century.

published by Burns & Oates

The Way of Chuang-Tzu

Thomas Merton describes this, his personal favourite of his books, as "not attempts at faithful reproduction but ventures in personal and spiritual interpretation." As free, interpretative readings, they are very much Merton's own, the result of five years of reading, study and meditation.

Chuang Tzu, the most spiritual of the classic Chinese philosophers, is the chief historical spokesman for Taoism. Through his writings and those of other Taoist sages, Indian Buddhism was transformed in China into what we now know by its Japanese name—Zen.

The Chinese sage abounds in wit, paradox, satire and shattering insight into the true ground of being. Merton here brings a vivid, modern idiom to the timeless wisdom of Tao.

Unavailable since the early 1980s, this little volume speaks immediately to the spiritual sensibilities of the 1990s.

Line drawings from The Tao Book of Painting add to its delight.

Thoughts on the East

The Eastern religious traditions, especially the varieties of Buddhism, were the last great passion in Thomas Merton's life. His participation in a monastic conference in Asia led to his premature, accidental death. He discoursed on equal terms with the Dalai Lama, and extracts from their interviews appear in this book.

George Woodcock, author of the highly acclaimed *Thomas Merton: Monk and Poet,* completed the introduction to this collection shortly before his own death. It brings together extracts from Merton's *Asian Journal* (Hinduism and varieties of Buddhism) and from other short works on Eastern religions written in the last few years of his life. They all combine to demonstrate the breadth of vision that is such an integral part of Merton's lasting appeal, his quest for a deeper unity underlying apparent fragmentation. They might be regarded as steps toward the great book on monasticism that Merton might have written but never did. As they stand, they provide Merton's essential definitions of the religions that so much interested him in the last years of his life, and of which he became the most skilful Western interpreter.

Thomas Merton: The Hermitage Years

JOHN HOWARD GRIFFIN

John Howard Griffin, the best-selling author of *Black Like Me*, here takes us inside the world of Thomas Merton. In this book, originally published under the title *Follow the Ecstasy*, he provides an intimate look at the last, critical years of Merton's life. This period coincided with the monk's long-sought permission to withdraw to a hermitage in the monastery grounds of Gethsemani.

The retreat to greater solitude, ironically, plunged Merton even more deeply into the life and turmoil of his times. In an extraordinary burst of spiritual and creative energy, he investigated the religions of the East, wrestled with the social and political issues of racism, war, and peace, and experienced anew the wonder and anguish of human love.

"I first read this book when I was actually living in Merton's hermitage in 1985. It still waits on my shelf filled with highlighted and rich memories, bits of forced and brutal truth, and ecstasies that he has taught me to follow. I return to it regularly, as if visiting a holy shrine to my soul—and his."—Richard Rohr, O.F.M. , Centre for Action and Contemplation

Burns & Oates publish books of general Christian interest as well as books on theology, scripture, spirituality and mysticism.
A free catalogue will be sent on request:
BURNS & OATES Dept A,
Wellwood, North Farm Road, Tunbridge Wells, Kent TN2 3DR
Tel: (01892) 510850 Fax: (01892) 515903